DUMPLINGS

DUMPLINGS

More than 70 delicious bite-size dumplings, buns & rolls

RYLAND PETERS & SMALL

Designer Paul Stradling
Editor Abi Waters
Production Manager Gordana Simakovic
Indexer Vanessa Bird

Published in 2026 by
Ryland Peters & Small
20–21 Jockey's Fields
London WC1R 4BW

www.rylandpeters.com
email: euregulations@rylandpeters.com

10 9 8 7 6 5 4 3 2 1

ISBN: 978-1-78879-776-4

Printed in China.

A CIP record for this book is available from the British Library.
US Library of Congress Cataloging-in-Publication data has been applied for.

FSC www.fsc.org
MIX
Paper | Supporting responsible forestry
FSC® C008047

The authorised representative in the EEA is Authorised Rep Compliance Ltd., Ground Floor, 71 Lower Baggot Street, Dublin, D02 P593, Ireland.
www.arccompliance.com

NOTES

• Both British (Metric) and American (Imperial ounces plus US cups) are included in these recipes for your convenience; however, it is important to work with one set of measurements only and not alternate between the two within a recipe.

• All spoon measurements are level unless otherwise specified.

• All eggs are medium (UK) or large (US), unless specified as large, in which case US extra-large should be used. Uncooked or partially cooked eggs should not be served to the very old, frail, young children, pregnant women or those with compromised immune systems.

• Ovens should be preheated to the specified temperatures. We recommend using an oven thermometer. If using a fan-assisted oven, adjust temperatures according to the manufacturer's instructions.

• When a recipe calls for the grated zest of citrus fruit, buy unwaxed fruit and wash well before using. If you can only find treated fruit, scrub well in warm soapy water before using.

CONTENTS

INTRODUCTION

Dumplings are proof that the best foods don't need to be complicated. Small, comforting and endlessly adaptable, they've been showing up in kitchens around the world for centuries – wrapped, folded, pleated and filled with whatever ingredients people had on hand. They're equal parts tradition and creativity, and somehow always feel like a treat.

But dumplings are also about the moment. Making them can be slow and mindful, a chance to switch off and work with your hands – or it can be lively and a little chaotic, with friends gathered around the table, everyone folding their own slightly imperfect creations.

This book brings together over 70 recipes to help you make dumplings your own way. We start with Basic Dough Recipes, because every great dumpling begins with the basics. Once you've got your dough down, everything else becomes easier (and way more fun).

From there, each chapter explores a different dumpling mood. Little Pockets is filled with classic dumplings and dim sum – small but mighty, packed with flavour and perfect for sharing (or not). Think savoury fillings wrapped in tender skins, ready to be steamed, boiled or pan-fried. Soft & Steamy is all about comfort, with fluffy bao and pillowy buns that feel like the food equivalent of a hug from your favourite person.

For those who love a bit of crunch, Crisp & Golden delivers. These are your fried and baked dumplings and rolls – crispy on the outside, rich and savoury on the inside and almost impossible to stop eating. Wrapped & Golden takes a broader view, bringing together filled parcels and rolls inspired by different corners of the world, perfect for when you want to experiment a little.

And because every dumpling deserves a finishing touch, the final chapter is dedicated to sauces, dips, drizzles and garnishes. These are the details that pull everything together – spicy, tangy, savoury or fresh – and let you customize every bite

This isn't a book about perfection. Your folds don't have to be neat, and your dumplings don't have to match. In fact, the slightly uneven ones are usually the best. It's about trying, tasting and enjoying the process as much as the result.

PYREX

BASIC DOUGH RECIPES

There are six basic dough recipes used in this book. The bread dough and fluffy bread dough are used to create filled steamed buns and clamshell bao, the rice flour dough is used for filled dumplings, the crystal skin dough to make beautiful almost-translucent dumplings, and the egg and wheat dough is used for delicious dim sum.

BREAD DOUGH

2 tsp easy-bake/rapid-rise dried yeast

450 g/3½ cups Asian white wheat flour

15 g/2 tbsp icing/confectioners' sugar, sifted

15 g/2 tbsp dried milk powder

¼ tsp salt

2 tsp baking powder

50 ml/3½ tbsp vegetable oil, plus extra for oiling the bowl

MAKES 16 SKINS

Place the yeast in a large mixing bowl, then add the flour, sugar, milk powder, salt and baking powder. Make sure the yeast is separated from the salt by the layer of flour. Add the oil and 180 ml/¾ cup water and bring together with a dough scraper. When no dry flour remains, remove the dough from the bowl and place on a lightly floured surface. Knead firmly for about 5–10 minutes, until smooth and elastic.

Lightly oil the mixing bowl. Shape the dough into two cylinders and place back in the oiled bowl, cover with oiled cling film/plastic wrap and leave in a warm place to rise for about 40–60 minutes, or until doubled in size.

Remove the risen dough from the bowl, punch it down and knead it again briefly, but very carefully rather than firmly this time. Roll out each dough ball so that it has a diameter of around 7.5 cm/3 inches; try to make the centre slightly thicker than the edges so that it can hold the filling. Cover each dough circle with a damp kitchen cloth as you finish to stop it from drying out.

EGG DOUGH

150 g/1 cup plus 2 tbsp Asian white wheat flour, plus extra for dusting

1 egg

MAKES 16 SKINS

Place the flour in a large mixing bowl and add the egg and 40 ml/scant 3 tablespoons water. Bring the mixture together, then turn the dough out onto a lightly floured surface. Using lightly floured hands, knead for 20–25 minutes. The dough will be sticky at first but should become smooth and silky.

Separate the dough in half and roll into two equal cylinders, about 2.5 cm/1 inch in diameter. Cover with a damp kitchen cloth to prevent it from drying out and set aside to rest for 30 minutes.

Use a sharp knife to slice the dough cylinders into 16 equal pieces. On a lightly floured surface, roll out each piece with a rolling pin until it has a neat round shape and a diameter of around 7.5 cm/3 inches.

CRYSTAL SKIN DOUGH

100 g/¾ cup wheat starch

50 g/½ cup tapioca starch

150 ml/⅔ cup boiling (not hot) water

salt

flour, for dusting

MAKES 16 SKINS

In a large mixing bowl, combine the wheat starch, tapioca starch and a pinch of salt. Add the boiling water and mix with a wooden spoon until a dough is formed.

Transfer to a lightly floured surface and knead until smooth. Separate the dough in half and roll into two equal cylinders, about 2.5 cm/1 inch in diameter.

Use the dough while it is still warm and pliable. Divide the dough into 16 equal balls. On a lightly floured surface use a rolling pin to roll the dough balls into thin discs, about 5 cm/2 inches in diameter. Cover the finished skins with a damp kitchen cloth as you work so that they don't dry out.

FLUFFY BREAD DOUGH

230 g/1¾ cups plain/all-purpose flour
3 tsp baking powder
2 tbsp caster/superfine sugar
80 ml/⅓ cup milk
3 tbsp groundnut/peanut oil
salt
flour, for dusting

MAKES 24 SKINS

Put the flour in a large bowl and mix in the baking powder, sugar and ½ teaspoon salt. Stir in the milk, oil and 70 ml/¼ cup plus 2 teaspoons water to form a dough.

Turn the dough onto a floured board and knead for 5 minutes until it becomes elastic. Cover with cling film/plastic wrap and let it rest at room temperature for 1 hour.

Divide and roll out the dough as instructed for the Bread Dough on page 9.

RICE FLOUR DOUGH

175 g/1⅓ cups plain/all-purpose flour, plus extra for dusting
125 g/1 cup minus 1 tbsp rice flour
250 ml/1 cup boiling (not hot) water
2 tbsp groundnut/peanut oil

MAKES 32 SKINS

Mix the two flours in a bowl, then stir in the boiling water and the oil. Stir until cool enough to handle, then knead to form a smooth mass. Use the dough while it is still warm and pliable. Divide and roll out the dough making 32 skins as instructed for the Crystal Skin Dough opposite.

WHEAT DOUGH

150 g/1 cup plus 2 tbsp Asian white wheat flour, plus extra for dusting

MAKES 16 SKINS

Make as for the Egg Dough (opposite left), omitting the egg and adding 80 ml/⅓ cup water instead.

LITTLE POCKETS

FILLED DUMPLINGS & DIM SUM

SALMON & SPRING ONION GYOZA

A classic gyoza filling of salmon and spring onions/scallions is completed perfectly by a punchy Japanese dipping sauce. Garnish with black sesame seeds if you have them for the perfect finishing touch.

250 g/9 oz. skinless salmon fillet, boned

2 spring onions/scallions, trimmed and thinly sliced

1 tbsp mirin

1 tbsp light soy sauce

20 gyoza wrappers

1 tbsp grapeseed oil

½ quantity Japanese dipping sauce (see page 113)

black sesame seeds and micro herbs, to serve

a baking sheet lined with baking parchment

SERVES 4

Begin by preparing the salmon. Cut the fillet into small cubes and put in a large mixing bowl. Add the spring onions, mirin and soy sauce, and stir well to combine.

Working one at a time, lay the gyoza wrappers out flat and place a teaspoon of the mixture on one half of each wrapper. Dampen the edges with a little cold water, fold the wrapper over the filling and carefully press the edges together to seal.

Preheat the oven to 110°C/225°F/Gas ¼ (or the lowest setting).

Heat the oil in a wok or large non-stick frying pan/skillet over a medium heat and fry half the gyoza on one side until really browned. Add 100 ml/⅓ cup water and simmer, partially covered, for 3 minutes until the water is evaporated. Fry for a further minute until crisp. Transfer the gyoza to the prepared baking sheet, turn off the oven and set in the still-warm oven while you cook the remaining gyoza in the same way.

Arrange the cooked gyoza on serving dishes and drizzle over the dipping sauce. Sprinkle with sesame seeds and micro herbs, and serve immediately.

PEA SHOOT & SHRIMP DUMPLINGS

1 batch Rice Flour Dough (see page 11)

extra fresh pea shoots or Chinese chives, to serve

dipping sauce of your choice, to serve

FILLING

250 g/5 small handfuls fresh pea shoots or mangetout/snowpeas, chopped

500 g/1 lb. 2 oz. raw prawns/shrimp, peeled, deveined and coarsely chopped (about 250 g/ 9 oz. prepared weight)

4-cm/1½-inch piece fresh ginger, peeled and grated

1 tbsp light soy sauce

1 tbsp Shaoxing (Chinese rice wine) or dry sherry (optional)

1 tsp sesame oil

1 egg white, beaten

MAKES 32

Pea shoots are leaf shoots of the mangetout, snowpea or garden pea. Sold in Chinese supermarkets and some greengrocers, they taste like essence of peas!

Put the pea shoots or mangetout in a colander and pour over boiling water, then quickly refresh under cold running water. Set aside.

Put the prawns in a bowl and mix in the ginger, light soy sauce, Shaoxing or sherry, sesame oil and egg white. Set aside for 15 minutes to allow the flavours to develop. Add the chopped pea shoots or mangetout.

Line the steamer basket with banana leaves (or use parchment paper).

Divide the dough into 32 pieces, roll into balls and cover with a damp cloth. Dust a dry surface with flour and, using a rolling pin, roll out a ball of dough to a circle, 8 cm/3 inch in diameter. Put a heaped teaspoon of filling in the centre, brush the edges with water, then bring them together to enclose the filling. Twist to seal and break off any excess dough. Repeat with the remaining dough and filling, keeping the dumplings covered as you make them.

Put the dumplings sealed-side down in the steamer basket, leaving space between them (cook in batches, if necessary).

Steam over boiling water for 7 minutes until the prawns are cooked through. Serve warm with extra pea shoots or Chinese chives and a dipping sauce of your choice.

DUMPLINGS WITH PEPPER SOY

The round dumpling wrappers for this variation on a Cantonese classic are available in the chilled sections of Chinese supermarkets. You can also use wonton wrappers, but they won't have the perfect, moon-white translucence of the real thing.

6 Chinese dried mushrooms

125 g/4 oz. cooked, peeled prawns/shrimp

150 g/5¼ oz. smoked streaky/fatty bacon

125 g/4 oz. skinless chicken breast

1 tbsp cornflour/cornstarch

1 tbsp groundnut/peanut oil

10 water chestnuts, finely diced

1 tbsp Shaoxing (Chinese rice wine) or dry sherry

1 tsp sugar

1 tsp sesame oil

1½ tbsp dark soy sauce

3-cm/1¼-inch piece fresh ginger, peeled and grated

50 dumpling wrappers (2 packs)

50 fresh coriander/cilantro leaves

TO SERVE

1 tbsp Japanese seven-spice (shichimi togarashi)

125 ml/½ cup dark soy sauce

MAKES 50

Put the mushrooms into a bowl and cover with boiling water for about 15 minutes to rehydrate. Drain and squeeze as dry as possible. Remove and discard the stems and any hard pieces. Chop the mushrooms finely and set aside.

Split the prawns in half lengthways, then cut them into pieces about 2 cm/¾ inch long. Set aside.

Chop the bacon and chicken and transfer to a small food processor. Add the cornflour and blend to a paste.

Put the oil into a wok and heat well, swirling the oil around the surface of the wok. Add the chicken paste and stir-fry, breaking up any lumps, until opaque. Add the mushrooms, water chestnuts, Shaoxing or dry sherry, sugar, sesame oil, soy sauce and grated ginger. Stir-fry until heated through, to mix the flavours, then let cool and chill until ready to assemble.

When ready to assemble, working on about 2–3 wrappers at a time and keeping the others covered, put 1 heaped teaspoon of the chicken mixture in the centre of a dumpling wrapper. Put a piece of prawn, red-side out, on one side of the filling, and a coriander leaf on the other side. Dip your finger in water and run it around the edge of the wrapper. Bring the edges of the wrapper together to form a half moon, then pleat the edges to form a crest. Tap the base of the moon on the work surface to flatten. Cover with a cloth until all the dumplings have been made.

Arrange in the steamer basket, making sure you leave space between the dumplings (cook in batches, if necessary).

Steam over boiling water for 9–10 minutes until done – the dough will become slightly translucent, letting the green coriander and red prawn show through.

To make the dipping sauce, stir the Japanese seven-spice into the soy. Serve the dumplings hot alongside the dipping sauce.

PULLED PORK & OLIVE DUMPLINGS

Slow-cooked pork flavoured with five-spice and paired with the savoury tang of olives is a modern take on an Asian classic that works so well.

1 batch Crystal Skin Dough (see page 10)

1-kg/2-lb. shoulder of pork from the neck-end, bone in (once cooked with bone and fat removed this should equate to roughly 250 g/ 9 oz. meat)

1 tbsp salt

1 tbsp dark muscovado sugar

2 tsp Chinese five-spice powder

35 g/⅓ cup black stoned/pitted olives, chopped

a roasting pan big enough for a shoulder of pork, lined with foil

a bamboo steamer, lined with parchment paper

MAKES 16

Preheat the oven to 220°C/425°F/Gas 7.

Place the pork shoulder in the foil-lined roasting pan and pat the meat dry with paper towels. Mix the dry ingredients together and rub into the pork. Wrap the shoulder in the foil, making sure that it is fully enclosed. Place the pork in the preheated oven. After 40 minutes, turn the heat down to 125°C/250°F/Gas ½ and cook for a further 4–6 hours until the pork is very tender. (Check occasionally during cooking time that the pork is not drying out; add a little water if it is.)

While the filling is cooking, prepare the crystal skin dough following the instructions from the basic recipe on page 10. Rest wrapped in cling film/plastic wrap until needed.

Once the meat has cooked, unwrap the joint, strain and set aside the juices. Remove the bone and fat from the meat and discard. Use a fork to pull the pork into shreds. Mix the chopped olives into the pulled pork and set aside to cool.

When the filling has cooled, roll out the skins. Place a large teaspoon of filling into the centre of each skin and gather the edges with your fingertips to make a round dumpling shape. Make small folds all the way around the top edge to create pleats. Pleat all the way around until the filling is enclosed.

Place the dumplings in the lined bamboo steamer over a high heat and steam for 15–20 minutes or until transparent. Just before serving, warm the pulled pork juices for dipping.

KIMCHI NOODLE DUMPLINGS

Korean fermented cabbage is often thought to be rather scary and even a little unpalatable, but in fact it is delicious, as are these crispy-bottomed dumplings. Feel free to adjust the spice levels in the kimchi recipe to your personal taste, or sample ready-made versions to find your favourite one.

150 g/⅔ cup minced pork

150 g/scant 1 cup cooked prawns/shrimp, peeled and very finely chopped

100 g/4 oz. Quick kimchi (see page 125)

2 tsp dark soy sauce

½ beaten egg

20 gyoza wrappers

4 tbsp vegetable oil

TO SERVE

1 quantity Choganjang (see page 114)

spring onions/scallions, thinly sliced

a baking sheet lined with baking parchment

SERVES 4

Put the pork, prawns, kimchi, soy sauce and beaten egg in a large mixing bowl and mix together until evenly combined.

Working one at a time, lay the gyoza wrappers out flat and place a teaspoon of the mixture on one half of each wrapper. Dampen the edges with a little cold water, fold the wrapper over the filling and carefully press the edges together to seal.

Preheat the oven to 110°C/225°F/Gas ¼ (or the lowest setting).

Heat the oil in a wok or large non-stick frying pan/skillet set over a high heat. Add half the dumplings and fry for about 1 minute until the bottoms are golden. Add 125 ml/½ cup water to the pan, cover and simmer for 5 minutes until the filling is heated through. Remove the lid and cook for a further 1–2 minutes until the bottoms are crispy. Transfer the dumplings to the prepared baking sheet, turn off the oven and set in the still-warm oven while you cook the remaining dumplings in the same way.

Arrange the dumplings on warmed plates and serve with the choganjang, scattered with spring onions.

DUMPLINGS WITH MAKRUT LIME & LEMONGRASS

2 garlic cloves, crushed/ minced

4-cm/1½-inch piece fresh galangal or ginger, peeled and finely chopped

2 stalks lemongrass, finely chopped

8 makrut lime leaves, finely chopped

2 hot Thai chillies/chiles, deseeded and finely chopped

12 shallots, finely chopped

4 tbsp fish sauce or light soy sauce

500 g/1 lb. 2 oz. skinless, boneless chicken breast, minced/ground

4 tbsp coconut cream

50 small fresh wonton wrappers (2 packs)

banana leaves, for steaming (optional)

sweet chilli/chile sauce, to serve

MAKES 50

South-east Asian flavours take centre stage in these pretty dumplings. They make perfect party food as they freeze well and look gorgeous served straight from bamboo steamers.

Using a small food processor or large mortar and pestle, grind the garlic, galangal or ginger, lemongrass, makrut lime leaves, chillies and shallots to form a paste – add a little of the fish sauce or soy sauce if needed. Transfer to a bowl, add the remaining fish or soy sauce, minced chicken and coconut cream and stir well.

Cut the wonton wrappers into rounds and discard the trimmings – keep them covered with a kitchen cloth so they don't dry out. Line the bamboo steamer with banana leaves (or parchment paper).

Put a wrapper on a dry surface and spread with a teaspoon of filling. Gather up the edges to form a basket shape, leaving the middle exposed. Drop it gently onto the work surface to flatten the bottom and settle the filling. Place in the steamer. Repeat until all are made, keeping the wrappers and the dumplings covered as you go and leaving space between the dumplings (cook in batches, if necessary).

Steam over boiling water for 8 minutes and serve immediately with sweet chilli sauce for dipping.

CRAB DUMPLNGS

These bite-size morsels are typical of Chinese dim sum – they look elegant, smell tantalizing and taste good! Use fresh crab meat for the very best flavour. If you do need to use frozen crab meat, make sure it is well drained before using.

125 g/4 oz. fresh crab meat

50 g/1¾ oz. cooked, peeled prawns/shrimp, chopped

4 canned water chestnuts, finely chopped

2 spring onions/scallions, finely chopped

2.5-cm/1-inch piece fresh ginger, peeled and grated

1 small chilli/chile, deseeded and finely chopped

1 tbsp chopped fresh coriander/cilantro

1 tbsp light soy sauce

20 x 8–9 cm/3½ inch round wonton wrappers

toasted sesame seeds, to garnish

dipping sauce of your choice, to serve

MAKES 20

In a bowl mix together the crab meat, prawns, water chestnuts, spring onions, ginger, chilli, coriander and soy sauce.

Brush the edges of a wonton wrapper with water. Place a heaped teaspoon of filling in the centre. Draw up the edges and press together. Repeat to make 20 dumplings. Cover until ready to cook.

Arrange the dumplings in the steamer basket lined with parchment paper, making sure they do not touch each other (cook in batches, if necessary).

Steam over boiling water for 5 minutes.

Sprinkle with toasted sesame seeds and serve with a dipping sauce.

CHICKEN & POTATO CREAM STEW DUMPLINGS

These tasty dumplings commemorate the classic taste of canned creamed chicken soup. The mild flavours mean that they would be a great way of introducing young children to dim sum.

1 batch Crystal Skin Dough (see page 10)

2 tbsp unsalted butter

½ onion, finely chopped

½ carrot, finely diced

½ celery stalk, finely diced

1 potato, peeled and finely diced

1 tbsp plain/all-purpose flour

1 chicken stock cube

175 ml/¾ cup milk

1 chicken breast, finely diced

½ tsp each salt and black pepper

melted butter, for dipping

a bamboo steamer, lined with parchment paper

MAKES 16

Prepare the crystal skin dough following the intructions from the basic recipe on page 10. Wrap in cling film/plastic wrap and rest until needed.

Melt the butter in a large pan over a medium heat. Add the diced onion, carrot, celery and potato. Cook, stirring occasionally, until tender, about 3–4 minutes.

Whisk in the flour slowly and heat for a minute. Next crumble the stock cube into the pan and gradually add the milk, whisking constantly. Continue cooking and stirring until the sauce has slightly thickened, about 1–2 minutes.

Add the chicken. Bring the sauce to a boil; reduce heat and simmer until the potatoes and chicken are tender, about 12–15 minutes. Set aside to cool.

While the filling is cooling, roll out the crystal skin dough following the intructions on page 10. Place a large teaspoon of filling into the centre of each skin. Fold the dumplings in half and pinch the edges together to form a simple crescent shape.

Space out the dumplings evenly in the bamboo steamer lined with parchment paper. Steam over boiling water for about 15–20 minutes or until the skins turn transparent. Serve warm with the hot melted butter for dipping.

SPICY CHICKEN & SHRIMP DUMPLINGS

1 batch Wheat Dough (see page 11)

1 chicken breast

60 g/2¼ oz. raw prawns/shrimp, peeled and deveined

1 leek, chopped

2 Chinese chive stalks, chopped

a large handful of fresh coriander/cilantro, chopped

½–1 tbsp Korean hot pepper powder (to taste)

1 tsp freshly ground black pepper

1 tbsp oyster sauce

½ tbsp sesame oil

DIPPING SAUCE

1 garlic clove, finely chopped

1 tbsp grated fresh ginger

6 tbsp soy sauce

2 tbsp chilli/chile oil

MAKES 16

The amount of hot pepper powder can be added more or less to taste in these delicious Korean dumplings.

Prepare the wheat dough following the instructions in the basic recipe on page 11, and rest wrapped in cling film/plastic wrap until needed. Meanwhile, mince the chicken breast and prawns using a sharp knife to very finely chop. Transfer to a mixing bowl and combine with the rest of the filling ingredients. Chill in the fridge for 30 minutes.

Roll out the skins, continuing to follow the basic recipe on page 11. Put a large teaspoon of filling into the centre of each skin. Dip your fingertips in a small dish of water and slightly moisten the edge of half the skin. Seal the dumpling up tightly using your fingers to pinch, pull and fold the skin into 4 pleats at the join. Repeat the process until all the mixture and skins have been used.

Bring a large pan of water to boiling point. Gently lower in the dumplings and cover with a lid to poach. The dumplings are cooked when they float to the top of the liquid.

To make the dipping sauce, mix together all the ingredients.

Drain the dumplings and serve at once accompanied with the dipping sauce.

Tip: If you prefer a crispy base, you can lightly pan-fry the uncooked dumplings in a small amount of oil and finish off the cooking by poaching in water or stock.

SCALLOP & CRAB DUMPLINGS

The scallop is the pearlescent jewel in the crown of these dumplings, which are great for impressing guests at a dinner party. The spicy lime-based dipping sauce is the perfect complement to the luxurious seafood filling.

1 batch Crystal Skin Dough (see page 10)

1 leek, finely chopped

60 g/2¼ oz. fresh crab meat, flaked

1 tsp minced fresh ginger

1 tesp crushed/minced garlic

½ tsp salt

½ tsp ground white pepper

½ tsp Shaoxing rice wine

½ tsp sugar

1 tsp oil

1 tsp cornflour/ cornstarch

16 scallops

DIPPING SAUCE

4 tbsp sugar

2 tbsp water

2 tbsp white vinegar

1 garlic clove, crushed/ minced

1 tbsp fish sauce

1 tsp Indonesian chilli/ chile sauce

juice of 2 limes

a handful of fresh coriander/cilantro, finely chopped

a bamboo steamer lined with parchment paper

MAKES 16

Begin by making the dipping sauce. Boil the sugar, water and vinegar in a small saucepan until the sugar has dissolved. Turn down the heat to medium, stir in the garlic, fish sauce and chilli sauce and simmer for 1 minute. Remove from the heat. Cool and add the lime juice and coriander. Set aside ready for later.

Prepare the crystal dough following the instructions on page 10.

While the dough is resting make the filling. In a bowl combine the leek, crab meat, ginger, garlic, seasoning, Shaoxing rice wine, sugar, oil and cornflour; mix well.

Roll out the crystal dough skins, continuing to follow the instructions on page 10. Put a large teaspoon of the crab mixture into the centre of each skin and place a scallop on the top. Fold the skin in half over the filling, and pinch together the sides to create the traditional crescent-shaped dumpling. Fold the two ends of the dumpling inwards so that they overlap.

Press together to seal and form the Chinese ingot shape.

Place the dumplings into the bamboo steamer lined with parchment paper. Steam over boiling water for 15–20 minutes or until the skin is transparent.

Serve the dumplings hot with the dipping sauce.

SALMON & MUSHROOM DUMPLINGS

Salmon is a popular ingredient in any cuisine. It works well with the light texture of a crystal skin dough, and the pink against the white is attractive.

1 batch Crystal Skin Dough (see page 10)

1 tbsp sunflower oil

1 oyster mushroom

1 bunch enoki mushrooms

3 shiitaki mushrooms

20 g/¼ cup chanterelle mushrooms

1 garlic clove, finely chopped

1 small salmon fillet

1 tbsp minced fresh ginger

1 Chinese chive stalk, white parts removed

chilli/chile oil, to serve

a small round pastry cutter

a bamboo steamer, lined with parchment paper

MAKES 12

Prepare the crystal skin dough following the basic recipe on page 10, and make the filling while the dough is resting.

Slice the mushrooms into small, even pieces. Heat the sunflower oil in a frying pan/skillet and fry the mushrooms and garlic over a medium heat until fragant. Set aside to cool, discarding any excess juice.

Roll out the crystal skin dough and stamp out 24 circles using the small round pastry cutter. Portion the salmon fillet into 12 pieces and cut the Chinese chives into 3-cm/2-inch lengths.

Place a salmon piece in the centre of a skin, add a sprinkle of minced ginger and a chive piece neatly on the top. Lastly, top with a teaspoon of the cooked mushrooms. Cover with another round skin and press around the edge to seal.

Place the dumplings into the lined bamboo steamer and steam over boiling water until transparent. Serve hot with chilli oil.

PUMPKIN & LEEK DUMPLINGS

Vegetables take centre-stage in these warming and golden pumpkin and leek parcels. The interior of the dumpling should be soft in texture, flavoured beautifully with Chinese chives, ginger and Sichuan pepper.

1 batch Egg Dough (see page 10)

100 g/3½ oz. firm tofu, drained and sliced into small cubes

a pinch of salt

40 g/¼ cup steamed pumpkin

1 leek, finely chopped

2 Chinese chive stalks, white parts removed, finely chopped

a handful of fresh coriander/ cilantro, chopped

1 tsp minced fresh ginger

2 Chinese cabbage leaves, finely chopped

1 tsp Sichuan pepper

1 tsp black pepper

2 tbsp vegetarian stir-fry sauce

2 tbsp sesame oil

black vinegar, for dipping

MAKES 16

Prepare the egg dough following the instructions in the basic recipe on page 10. While the dough is resting, make the filling. Lightly salt the tofu slices and set them aside for 30 minutes, before squeezing out the excess water.

In a large bowl, mix together the steamed pumpkin with the tofu, chopped vegetables, coriander, ginger, Sichuan pepper, black pepper, vegetarian stir-fry sauce and sesame oil. Chill in the fridge for 30 minutes.

Roll out the egg dough, continuing to follow the instructions on page 10. Put a large teaspoon of filling into the centre of each skin. Dab a little water on one edge of the skin, fold in half over the filling and pinch the corners together to seal. Fold small pleats to seal up the middle. Continue with the rest of the batch, leaving the prepared dumplings on a tray lightly dusted with flour and covered with a damp kitchen cloth as you work.

Put a large pan of water on to boil. Lower the dumplings into the boiling water and cover with a lid. As soon as they start to float, they are cooked. Serve hot with black vinegar for dipping.

Tip: Alternatively, you can lightly pan-fry the uncooked dumpling and finish off the cooking by poaching the dumplings in a little stock or water.

TOFU, SUNDRIED TOMATO & OLIVE DUMPLINGS

pictured on page 2

Sun-kissed mediterranean ingredients fill this stylish little dumpling.

1 batch Wheat Dough (see page 11)

200 g/7 oz. firm tofu, drained and sliced into small cubes

a pinch of salt

1 leek, thinly sliced

60 g/½ cup sundried tomatoes, finely chopped

50 g/scant ½ cup black pitted olives, finely chopped

2 button mushrooms, finely chopped

2 Chinese chive stalks, white parts removed and finely chopped

a handful of fresh Chinese parsley, finely chopped

1 tsp Sichuan pepper

1 tsp black pepper

2 tbsp vegetarian stir-fry sauce

2 tbsp sesame oil

DIPPING SAUCE

1 tbsp aged balsamic vinegar

2 tbsp olive oil

a red shallot, finely chopped

a handful of fresh basil leaves, finely chopped

MAKES 16

Sprinkle a little salt over the tofu slices and set them aside for 30 minutes before squeezing out the excess water.

Prepare the wheat dough following the instructions from the basic recipe on page 11. While the dough is resting, prepare the filling. In a bowl combine the tofu with the chopped vegetables, parsley, seasonings, vegetarian stir-fry sauce and sesame oil. Mix well and place in the fridge for 30 minutes to chill.

Roll out the skins, continuing to follow the recipe on page 11. Put a large teaspoon of filling into the centre of a skin. Dip your fingertips in a small dish of water and slightly moisten the edge of half the skin. Fold in half and pinch the edges together to form a simple cresent shape. Fold the two ends of the dumpling together and overlap to create a Chinese ingot shape. Seal with another dab of water if needed. Repeat until all the mixture and skins have been used.

Gently lower the dumplings into a pan of boiling water and cover with a lid. As soon as the dumplings start to float they should be ready. Alternatively, you can lightly pan-fry the boiled dumplings to make the bottoms crispy and golden.

To make the dipping sauce, mix the ingredients together in a small bowl. Serve the dumplings hot with the dipping sauce on the side.

PORK & LEEK JIAOZI

pictured on page 12

Traditional jiaozi are extremely popular at holiday celebrations such as Chinese New Year. Often prepared in an assembly line by various family members, these tasty dumplings are enjoyed by children and adults alike. The folded, plump pleated shape is a nice easy one to start with.

1 batch Wheat Dough (see page 11)

100 g/3½ oz. firm tofu, drained and sliced into small cubes

a pinch of salt

100 g/3½ oz. minced/ground pork

2 Chinese chive stalks, white parts removed, finely chopped

a large handful of fresh coriander/cilantro, chopped

1 tsp Sichuan pepper

1 tsp black pepper

2 tbsp dark soy sauce

2 tbsp sesame oil

1 leek, finely chopped

2 button mushrooms, finely chopped

1 tbsp sunflower oil

black vinegar, for dipping

MAKES 16

Prepare the wheat dough following the instructions from the basic recipe on page 11. While the dough is resting, begin the filling. Sprinkle the tofu slices with salt and set aside for 30 minutes before squeezing out the excess water.

In a large bowl mix the pork with the tofu and the rest of the ingredients apart from the sunflower oil and black vinegar.

Roll out the skins, continuing to follow the instructions from the recipe on page 11. Place a small tablespoon of filling neatly into the centre of a skin. Dip your fingertips into a small dish of water and slightly moisten the edge of half the skin. Fold the skin in half over the filling. Pinch one end together and make small folds to form pleats. The end result should be a plump sealed pocket. Tap the dumplings base-down on your work surface to finish. As you are working, set aside the finished dumplings on a floured baking sheet under a damp cloth so they do not dry out.

Heat the sunflower oil over a medium heat in a large frying pan/skillet. Lightly fry the dumplings until golden brown on the bottom. To finish off the cooking process, place the dumplings in a large pan of boiling water. Cover with a lid and poach until they float to the surface.

Serve the dumplings hot with black vinegar for dipping.

PORK & CABBAGE SHUMAI

1 batch Egg Dough (see page 10)

100 g/3½ oz. raw prawns/shrimp, peeled and deveined

100 g/3½ oz. lean minced/ground pork

60 g/1¼ cups chopped cabbage

1 tbsp oyster sauce

½ tbsp sesame oil

1 tsp ground white pepper

1 tbsp cornflour/cornstarch

1 tsp salt

toasted white sesame seeds, to garnish

DIPPING SAUCE

125 ml/½ cup soy sauce

2 tbsp sesame oil

a large handful of fresh coriander/cilantro, chopped

2 spring onions/scallions, sliced

1 tsp crushed/minced garlic

1 tbsp grated fresh ginger

a bamboo steamer, lined with parchment paper

MAKES 16

Create the flower shape for these pretty bite-size dumplings by lightly squeezing the egg dough cup in the middle.

Prepare the egg dough following the instructions from the basic recipe on page 10. While the dough is resting, make the filling. Mince the prawns using a sharp knife to finely chop into small pieces. Transfer to a large mixing bowl, add the rest of the filling ingredients and mix thoroughly.

Roll out the egg dough, continuing to follow the instructions from the recipe on page 10. To assemble the shumai, place a wrapper on your palm and add a small tablespoon of filling to the centre. Gather the edges of the wrapper and gently pleat so that a basket shape is formed up and around the filling, leaving the middle exposed. Lightly tap the base of the dumpling on a countertop to flatten the bottom and make sure the filling fills the nooks and crannies. Lightly squeeze the middle with your thumb and forefinger to create the classic flower shape. Repeat for the rest of the wrappers and filling.

Arrange the shumai at the bottom of the lined bamboo steamer, leaving plenty of space between each one. Cover and steam the dumplings over boiling water for 7 minutes or until cooked through.

Make the dipping sauce while the dumplings are steaming by stirring the ingredients together in a small bowl.

Remove the dumplings from the steamer using the parchment paper to assist. Serve warm sprinkled with toasted white sesame seeds and alongside the dipping sauce.

WONTON PORK MONEYBAGS

These can be cooked and served in bamboo steamers. If you cook three tiers at a time, you can serve the first batch while the next one is cooking. The bacon isn't a traditional Chinese ingredient, but it means you need less salt.

500 g/1 lb. 2 oz. minced/ground pork

125 g/1 cup raw prawns/shrimp, peeled and deveined

3 slices smoked streaky/fatty bacon, chopped

1 tsp crushed pepper, preferably Szechuan

1 egg white

2 tsp sesame oil

3-cm/1½-inch piece fresh ginger, peeled and grated

1 garlic clove, crushed/minced

2 tsp cornflour/cornstarch

4 spring onions/scallions

4 canned water chestnuts, finely diced

1 Chinese snake/yard-long bean or 4 green/French beans, thinly sliced

50 small fresh wonton wrappers (2 packs)

salt

banana leaves, for steaming (optional)

soy sauce, to serve

MAKES 50

Put the pork, prawns and bacon into a food processor and blend to a purée. With the motor running, add the pepper, egg white, sesame oil, ginger, garlic, cornflour and 2 teaspoons salt.

Finely chop the white and green parts of the spring onions crossways, transfer to a mixing bowl, then add the pork mixture, water chestnuts and bean(s). Mix well – using your hands is the best way.

Cut the wonton wrappers into rounds and discard the trimmings – keep them covered with a damp kitchen cloth so they don't dry out. Line the steamer basket with banana leaves (or parchment paper).

Put a tablespoon of the pork filling in the centre of each round wrapper. Use a teaspoon to smooth the mixture almost to the edges.

Cup the wonton in the palm of your hand. Gather up your hand, pushing down with the teaspoon: you will achieve an open-topped, pleated, money-bag-shaped container filled with mixture. Drop it gently onto the work surface to flatten the bottom and settle the filling. Place in the steamer. Repeat until all the dumplings are made, keeping the wrappers and the dumplings covered as you go and leaving space between the dumplings (cook in batches, if necessary).

Steam over boiling water for about 7–10 minutes, or until cooked through. Serve hot with a simple soy sauce dip.

SOFT & STEAMY

BAO & PILLOWY BUNS

BARBECUE PORK STEAMED BUNS

The pillowy-soft bread bun surrounding sweet and sticky char siu-style pork is just a heavenly combination. Traditionally, the filling for this type of steamed bun uses up leftovers from dinner the night before, but you can make the filling using fresh pork, as here.

1 batch Bread Dough (see page 9)

FILLING

1 tbsp sunflower or vegetable oil

1 shallot, chopped

2 tbsp dry sherry

350 g/12 oz. pork loin, diced

1 tsp crushed/minced garlic

2 tbsp clear honey

2 tbsp hoisin sauce

1 tsp Chinese five-spice powder

1 tbsp light soy sauce

MAKES 16

To make the filling, heat the oil in a pan over a medium heat and add the shallot. Cook over a medium heat until softened and lightly caramelized, about 5–7 minutes. Pour in the sherry and let the alcohol cook out for a few minutes. Lower the heat a little and add the pork. Cook, stirring, for a further 2 minutes or until lightly browned.

Meanwhile, in a separate bowl, mix the garlic, honey, hoisin sauce, Chinese five-spice powder and soy sauce with about 2 tablespoons water. Add this to the pork and shallot mixture. Stir well. Cover and cook over a low heat for 1 hour, or until the sauce has thickened and the pork is tender. Check occasionally during cooking to ensure the sauce does not dry out. Add a little extra water if necessary.

Divide the bread dough into 16 portions and roll out each dough ball to 7.5 cm/3 inch in diameter (try to make the centre slightly thicker than the edges so that it can hold the filling). Cover each dough circle with a damp kitchen cloth as you finish to stop it from drying out.

Allow the pork mixture to cool and finely chop the meat.

Place a heaped tablespoon of the filling in the centre of each dough circle. Gather the edges to form pleats and pinch to seal the top of the bun.

Cut out 16 squares of parchment paper just larger than the buns. Place a bun on each square of parchment and then place into the steamer basket at least 5 cm/2 inches apart. You may have to do this in batches depending on the size of your steamer. Cover with oiled cling film/plastic wrap and allow to rise for 30 minutes.

Steam over boiling water for 8–10 minutes until the dough is light and fluffy. Allow to cool slightly, then serve.

LITTLE SZECHUAN CHICKEN STEAMED BUNS

Traditionally filled with pork or bean paste, these fluffy buns are a popular and comforting dim sum option. For a whiter bun, you can replace half the flour with potato flour, but the dough is less elastic, so harder to handle.

1 batch Fluffy Bread Dough (see page 11)

FILLING

4 chicken thighs

3 tbsp dark soy sauce

2 tbsp clear honey

1 tbsp Shaoxing (Chinese rice wine) or dry sherry

1–2 tbsp hot chilli/chile sauce

2–3 garlic cloves, crushed/minced

1 tbsp Szechuan peppercorns, crushed

MAKES 24

Put the chicken in a baking dish. Put the soy sauce in a bowl, mix in the honey, Shaoxing or sherry, chilli sauce, garlic and peppercorns, add to the chicken and turn to coat. Cover with foil or a lid and place in the fridge to marinate for 30 minutes–2 hours.

Preheat the oven to 180°C/350°F/Gas 4.

Transfer the baking dish, still covered, to the preheated oven and roast for 20 minutes, then uncover and cook a further 20 minutes until cooked through. Let cool, then remove the meat from the bones, shred it finely and mix the shredded meat with any marinade and juices left in the dish.

Divide the dough into 24 pieces and cover with a damp cloth. Take each piece of dough and, using your fingers, shape into a 6-cm/2½-inch disc. Put a teaspoon of the chicken filling in the centre of each one and gather up the dough around it. Pinch the edges together and twist to seal.

Place the buns, sealed edges up, on a sheet of parchment that will fit in your steamer, or on 24 individual parchment squares, then place them into the steamer basket at least 2.5 cm/1 inch apart. You may have to do this in batches depending on the size of your steamer. Steam over boiling water for 15–20 minutes until the buns are light and fluffy. Allow to cool slightly, then serve.

RED CURRY CHICKEN & LENTIL BAO

A taste of Thailand fused with traditional Chinese bao (or baozi to give them their full name) in these beautiful red curry buns.

- 1 batch Bread Dough (see page 9)
- 2 tbsp sunflower oil
- 2 onions, finely sliced
- 2 garlic cloves, crushed/minced
- 1–2 tbsp Thai red curry paste (to taste)
- 2 chicken breasts, cut into bite-size pieces
- 500 ml/2 cups hot chicken stock
- 80 g/scant ½ cup dried red lentils

a bamboo steamer, lined with parchment paper

MAKES 16

Make the bread dough following the instructions in the basic recipe on page 9. While the dough is rising, prepare the filling.

Heat 1 tablespoon of the oil in a large frying pan/skillet and add the onions. Cook for 3 minutes over a gentle heat until soft and fragrant. Stir in the crushed/minced garlic and curry paste and cook for 1–2 minutes more.

Add the chicken pieces and cook for 2–3 minutes. Stir in the stock and lentils, bring to the boil, cover and simmer for 25 minutes, stirring occasionally, until the lentils are tender and the chicken is cooked. Set aside to cool.

Continue to follow the instructions from the bread dough recipe on page 9. Once the skins are ready, place 1 tablespoon of the filling in the centre of each round. Gather and pleat the edges, pinching to seal the top of the bun.

Set the finished buns in the lined bamboo steamer about 5 cm/2 inches apart. You may have to do this in batches depending on the size of your steamer. Cover with oiled cling film/plastic wrap and allow to rise for another 30 minutes.

Once risen, steam the bao over a high heat for 15–20 minutes or until the dough is light and fluffy. Cool slightly and serve.

CHAR SIU STEAMED BUNS

If you live near a Chinatown market, you can buy their delicious barbecued pork, char siu. If you don't, try the home-style version given below, reserving a little for the buns.

½ batch Fluffy Bread Dough (see page 11)

FILLING

1 tbsp groundnut/peanut oil

1 tbsp chopped onion

1 garlic clove, crushed/minced

125 g/4 oz. Chinese barbecued pork (char siu), finely chopped (see right)

2 spring onions/scallions, chopped, plus extra to serve (optional)

1 tbsp light soy sauce

black pepper

½ tsp sugar

¼ tsp sesame oil

MAKES 8

Heat the oil in a wok over a high heat, add the onion and garlic and stir-fry until golden. Add the pork, spring onions/scallions, soy sauce, pepper, sugar and sesame oil, stir-fry quickly over a high heat, then reduce the heat and simmer gently for about 5 minutes. Let cool.

Turn out the dough onto a work surface and knead for 5 minutes. Divide into eight portions, then roll each piece into a ball and flatten to a disc. Put one-eighth of the filling in the middle of each disc, then gradually work the outside edge of the disc around and over the top to enclose the filling. Seal.

Cut out eight squares of parchment paper, about 10-cm/4-inch square. Place a bun on each square of parchment and then place into the steamer basket at least 5 cm/2 inches apart. You may have to do this in batches depending on the size of your steamer. Steam over simmering water for about 30 minutes, until well puffed. Allow to cool slightly, then serve with some extra chopped spring onions, if you like.

CHINESE BARBECUE PORK

Cut 1 kg/2 lb. 4 oz. pork fillet/tenderloin into two long strips lengthways. Rub with 1 tablespoon black pepper and 1 tablespoon Chinese five-spice powder. Put 4 tablespoons soy sauce into a shallow dish and stir in 2 teaspoons sesame oil. Add the pork and turn to coat well. Cover and chill overnight.

Next day, let return to room temperature for 1 hour, then cook on a barbecue/outdoor grill or roast on a rack in a preheated oven at 200°C/400°F/Gas 6 for about 15 minutes. Reduce the heat to 180°C/350°F/Gas 4 and continue roasting for about 20 minutes. Let rest for 20 minutes before cutting.

STEAMED BUNS FILLED WITH SPICY MALA LAMB & MINT

This Szechuan-inspired minced/ground lamb filling is rich with warming cumin, ground coriander and Szechuan pepper, which marries beautifully with the fragrant fresh mint.

1 batch Bread Dough (see page 9), but add 1 tsp ground Szechuan pepper with the flour

FILLING

200 g/7 oz. minced/ ground lamb

1 leek, chopped

60 g/2 oz. preserved spicy mustard stems, chopped

3 garlic cloves, chopped

20 g/¾ oz. fresh ginger, peeled and chopped

2 long red chillies/chiles (deseeded if you don't want it too hot), chopped

60 g/2 oz. fresh mint leaves, thinly sliced

60 g/2 oz. courgette/ zucchini, finely chopped

2 tbsp light soy sauce

2 tbsp Shaoxing (Chinese rice wine) or dry sherry

1 tbsp ground cumin

2 tsp ground coriander

2 tbsp groundnut/ peanut oil

1 tbsp cornflour/ cornstarch

½ tbsp ground Szechuan pepper, or to taste

salt

MAKES 16

Put the lamb into a bowl and add all the other filling ingredients and 2 teaspoons salt. Mix well, cover and place in the fridge to marinate for at least 2 hours.

Divide the bread dough into 16 portions and roll out each dough ball to 7.5 cm/3 inch in diameter (try to make the centre slightly thicker than the edges so that it can hold the filling). Cover each dough circle with a damp kitchen cloth as you finish to stop it from drying out.

Divide the lamb filling into 16 portions and place a portion into the centre of each dough circle. Gather the dough to form pleats and pinch to seal the top of the bun.

Cut out 16 squares of parchment paper just larger than the buns. Place a bun on each square of parchment and then place into the steamer basket at least 5 cm/2 inches apart.

You may have to do this in batches depending on the size of your steamer. Cover with oiled cling film/plastic wrap and allow to rise for 30 minutes.

Steam over boiling water for 8–10 minutes until the dough is light and fluffy. Allow to cool slightly, then serve.

FRIED SHRIMP & SCALLOP BAO

These bread buns are intensely delicious yet classy comfort food. With the surprise of a whole scallop in the centre, they are sure to be a winner. Separate dipping sauces are not usually needed with bread buns such as these as the filling inside should be juicy enough.

1 batch Bread Dough (see page 9)

2 spring onions/scallions, chopped

¼ head of cabbage, chopped

400 g/14 oz. raw prawns/shrimp, peeled and deveined

3 tbsp oyster sauce

2 tbsp Korean chilli flakes/hot pepper flakes

1 tbsp sesame oil

2 tbsp Shaoxing rice wine

16 scallops

a bamboo steamer, lined with parchment paper

MAKES 16

Make the bread dough following the instructions on page 9, leave to rise while you prepare the filling.

Mix the spring onions and cabbage together in a large bowl. Mince the prawns by chopping them very finely with a sharp knife. Add these to the vegetables along with the oyster sauce, chilli flakes, sesame oil and Shaoxing rice wine. Mix together well and chill in the fridge.

Continue to follow the instructions from the bread dough recipe on page 9. Once the skins are ready, place 1 tablespoon of the prawn filling in the centre and a scallop on top. Pull and pleat the edges of the dough to enclose the filling and pinch to seal the tops of the buns.

Set the buns in the lined bamboo steamer about 5 cm/2 inches apart. You may have to do this in batches depending on the size of your steamer. Cover with oiled cling film/plastic wrap and let rise for a final 30 minutes.

Steam the buns over boiling water for 8–10 minutes until the dough is light and fluffy. Let cool slightly and serve.

GARLIC PORK BAO BUNS

These pillowy bao buns contrast beautifully with the gutsy, succulent braised pork, making these a memorably tasty treat.

BRAISED PORK

1 tbsp olive oil

1 onion, finely chopped

2 garlic cloves, chopped

2-cm/¾-inch fresh ginger, peeled and chopped

400 g/14 oz. pork belly, cut into 2.5-cm/1-inch cubes

1 tbsp doenjang (Korean fermented soy bean paste)

1 tbsp gochujang (Korean chilli/chile paste)

1 tbsp dark soy sauce

1 tbsp rice wine or medium sherry

1 tsp white sugar

300 ml/1¼ cups chicken stock or water

BAO BUNS

250 g/1¾ cups plain/all-purpose flour

2 tsp white sugar

½ tsp fast-action dried/easy bake yeast

½ tsp baking powder

¼ tsp salt

100 ml/⅓ cup hand-hot water

50 ml/3½ tbsp whole milk

2 tsp white wine vinegar

shredded carrot and spring onion/scallion, to garnish

a large frying pan/skillet or casserole dish with a lid

a bamboo steamer, lined with non-stick baking parchment

MAKES 8

First make the braised pork. Heat the oil in the large, lidded frying pan/skillet or casserole dish. Fry the onion, garlic and ginger for 2 minutes, stirring, until the onion has softened. Add the chopped pork belly and fry, stirring often, until the pork is lightly browned.

Add the soy bean and chilli pastes and mix to coat thoroughly. Add the soy sauce, rice wine and sugar and cook, stirring, for 1 minute. Next, add the stock or water and bring to the boil.

Cover with a lid, reduce the heat and simmer for 1 hour until the pork is tender. Uncover the pan, increase the heat to bring the liquid to the boil and cook uncovered over medium heat, stirring often, until the sauce has considerably reduced. Set aside until needed.

Meanwhile, to make the bao, mix together the flour, sugar, yeast, baking powder and salt in a large bowl. Add in the hand-hot water, milk and vinegar and mix together to form a soft dough. Knead for about 10 minutes until the dough is supple and smooth.

Place the dough in an oiled bowl, cover with oiled cling film/plastic wrap and set aside in a warm place for an hour to rise.

On a lightly floured surface, knock back the risen ough and roll to form a thick sausage shape. Cut into 8 even-sized pieces and shape each piece into a ball. Roll each ball into an oval, roughly 12-cm/ 5-inches long. Fold each oval in half over a small rectangular piece of baking parchment. Cover with oiled cling film/plastic wrap and set aside to rest for 20 minutes.

Steam the buns in batches in the bamboo steamer, spaced apart, for about 10 minutes or until cooked through. Handling the hot buns carefully, remove the baking parchment.

Reheat the braised pork until piping hot, if needed, and fill each bun with braised pork, garnish with shredded carrot and spring onion/scallion and serve at once.

CLAMSHELL BAO WITH CHICKEN TERIYAKI

The chicken teriyaki filling is best when left to marinate in the fridge for 48 hours, so you need to start this recipe 2 days before you plan to cook it.

1 batch Bread Dough (see page 9)

CHICKEN TERIYAKI

5 chicken breasts or boneless chicken thighs

1 tbsp dark soy sauce

1 tbsp mirin

1 tbsp cooking sake

2 tbsp soy sauce

2 tbsp clear honey

3 garlic cloves, chopped

salt and black pepper

TO SERVE

10 Little Gem/Bibb lettuce leaves

20 tomato slices

shredded spring onions/scallions

MAKES 10

Slice the chicken breasts or thighs across the grain into ten slices in total, then place into a casserole with all the other chicken teriyaki ingredients, 1 teaspoon salt, 1 tablespoon ground black pepper and 125 ml/½ cup water. Mix well, cover and place in the fridge to marinate for 48 hours.

When ready to cook, preheat the oven to 190°C/375°F/Gas 5.

Remove the lid or cover from the chicken and roast in the preheated oven for 20 minutes until cooked through (reduce the oven temperature slightly if the chicken is browning too much). Allow to cool.

Cut some parchment paper into ten rectangles, 7 x 4 cm/2¾ x 1½ inches in size. Divide the bread dough into ten portions Roll out each portion of dough into an oval shape about 1 cm/½ in. thick, then fold in half, placing a parchment rectangle in-between the folded dough.

Cut another ten squares of paper just larger than the buns. Place a bun on each square, on its side, then place them into the steamer basket at least 5 cm/2 inches apart. You may have to do this in batches depending on the size of your steamer. Cover with oiled cling film/plastic wrap and leave to rise for 15 minutes.

Steam over boiling water for 10 minutes until the buns are light and fluffy. Allow to cool before serving.

To serve, place one lettuce leaf and two slices of tomato into each bun, then add a piece of chicken and some shredded spring onions.

CLAMSHELL BAO WITH MISO SALMON *pictured on page 44*

Delicate salmon marinated in miso, mirin, sake and honey makes the perfect filling for these soft clamshell buns.

1 batch Bread Dough (see page 9), but replace Asian white wheat flour with Asian wholemeal wheat flour (add 15% more water if using regular wholemeal flour)

MISO SALMON

10 portions salmon fillet, about 6 cm/2½ in. in length

1 tbsp miso paste

1 tbsp mirin

1 tbsp cooking sake

1 tbsp clear honey

1 tbsp ground black pepper

TO SERVE

4 ripe avocados, pitted and peeled

10 Little Gem/Bibb lettuce leaves

1 small red onion, sliced

MAKES 10

Place the salmon portions into a casserole with the other miso salmon ingredients and 125 ml/½ cup water. Mix well, cover and place in the fridge for at least 4 hours to marinate.

When ready to cook, preheat the oven to 180°C/350°F/Gas 4.

Remove the lid or cover from the casserole and cook the fish in the preheated oven for 15 minutes until cooked through (reduce the oven temperature slightly if the salmon is browning too much). Allow to cool while you prepare the buns.

Cut some parchment paper into ten rectangles, 7 x 4 cm/ 2¾ x 1½ inches in size. Divide the bread dough into ten portions. Roll out each portion of dough into an oval shape about 1 cm/½ inches thick, then fold in half, placing a parchment rectangle in-between the folded dough.

Cut another ten squares of parchment paper just larger than the buns. Place a bun on each square, on its side, then place them into the steamer basket at least 5 cm/2 inches apart. You may have to do this in batches depending on the size of your steamer. Cover with oiled cling film/plastic wrap and leave to rise for 15 minutes.

Steam over boiling water for 10 minutes until the buns are light and fluffy. Allow to cool before serving.

Slice the avocados and divide into ten portions.

To serve, place a lettuce leaf, avocado portion and a few red onion slices into each bun and top with the miso salmon.

CHINESE VEGETABLE CLAMSHELL BUNS

The fashionable clamshell shape of these buns shows off the vibrant colours of the vegetables. Take care with preparation as your knife skills will be on show. These buns are also good stuffed with the barbecue pork on page 46.

1 batch Bread Dough (see page 9)

1 head of Chinese cabbage leaves

3 handfuls Chinese spinach

2 small leeks

1 carrot, peeled and grated

8 oyster mushrooms, sliced

3 Chinese chive stalks, white parts removed, sliced

2 tbsp sunflower oil, plus extra for oiling the dough

a large handful of fresh coriander/cilantro, finely chopped

vegetarian stir-fry sauce, to serve

a bamboo steamer, lined with parchment paper

MAKES 16

Prepare, rise and roll out the bread dough following the instructions in the basic recipe on page 9.

Divide the dough into 16 round balls and flatten each slightly with a rolling pin into an oval shape, around 12 x 6 cm/ 4½ x 2⅓ inches. Cut parchment paper into 16 squares, each 12 cm/4½ inches. Use your fingers to lightly oil the surface of a piece of dough, place a square of paper on top and fold the dough in half so that the paper is in the centre. Cut another 16 squares of parchment paper just larger than the buns. Lay the paper squares on a tray and lightly dust with flour. Place a bun on top of each square on its side, cover with oiled cling film/ plastic wrap and leave to rise for 30–40 minutes.

While the buns are rising, slice the cabbage leaves, spinach and leeks lengthwise into ribbons approximately 6 cm/2¼ inches long and 2 cm/¾ inch thick. Set aside.

Brush the top of each risen bun lightly with sunflower oil. Lift the buns on their squares and place in the bamboo steamer about 4 cm/1½ inches apart. Steam over boiling water for 15–20 minutes until light and fluffy.

Heat the sunflower oil in a wok and stir-fry all the vegetables and herbs for around 2–3 minutes. Add vegetarian stir-fry sauce to taste and give the vegetables a quick toss.

When the buns are ready, remove the parchment paper from the middle of each one and fill with the hot vegetables. Serve.

生ものですから
お早めに召し上りください。

CRISP & GOLDEN

FRIED & BAKED DUMPLINGS & ROLLS

CHINESE POT STICKERS

Not to be confused with wontons, pot stickers, as they are called in North America, are a form of Chinese dumpling that is fried, steamed and then fried again so they are at once both soft and crispy. Use a non-stick frying pan/skillet to make these rather than a wok as you need an even base for the oil to settle.

125 g/2 cups finely chopped Chinese cabbage

1 tsp salt

1 leek, trimmed and finely chopped

2 garlic cloves, crushed

2 tbsp chopped fresh coriander/cilantro

250 g/1 cup minced/ground pork

24 gyoza wrappers

2 tbsp vegetable oil

Chinese Dipping Sauce (see page 113), to serve

garlic chive flowers or fresh chives, to garnish (optional)

a baking sheet lined with baking parchment

SERVES 4

Put the cabbage in a large mixing bowl with the salt and toss well to coat. Transfer to a colander and leave to drain for 1 hour to remove as much water as possible from the cabbage. Squeeze out any remaining water and put the cabbage in a clean large mixing bowl with the leek, garlic and coriander. Gradually work in the minced pork until combined.

Working one at a time, lay the gyoza wrappers out flat and place a teaspoon of the mixture on one half of each wrapper. Dampen the edges with a little cold water, fold the wrapper over the filling and carefully press the edges together to seal.

Preheat the oven to 110°C/225°F/Gas ¼ (or the lowest setting).

Heat 1 tablespoon of the oil in a wok or large non-stick frying pan/skillet set over a high heat. Add half the dumplings and fry for about 1 minute until the bottoms are golden. Add 100 ml/⅓ cup water and simmer, partially covered, for 5 minutes, until the water has evaporated. Cook for a further 2–3 minutes until the bottoms are crispy. Transfer the dumplings to the prepared baking sheet, turn off the oven and set in the still-warm oven while you cook the remaining dumplings in the same way.

Arrange the dumplings on plates and serve drizzled with the dipping sauce. Garnish with chive flowers, if using, and serve.

SHRIMP & MANGO WONTONS

Deep-fried golden crispy wontons are a moreish pleasure to eat. The tropical mango dipping sauce provides a sweet and sharp tang to cut through the savouriness of the skin. Folding in this rustic way is simple to do but the finish is very effective.

350 g/12½ oz. fresh prawns/shrimp, peeled and deveined

1 tsp salt

1 tsp black pepper

a small handful of fresh coriander/cilantro, chopped

50 g/1¾ oz. firm tofu, drained and sliced

1 packet of 16 wonton wrappers

sunflower oil, for deep-frying

DIPPING SAUCE

4 tbsp mayonnaise

2 tsp condensed milk

¼ small mango, diced into small cubes

MAKES 16

Use a pestle and mortar to mince the prawns to a fine paste. Season with the salt and pepper and mix in the coriander. Squeeze any excess water from the tofu, mash with a fork and add to the paste, stir well.

Hold a wonton skin on the palm of your hand and add a heaped teaspoon of filling to the centre. Dab the edges of the skin with a tiny bit of water and gather and scrunch the sides together in a rustic fashion. Repeat until all the filling and skins are used.

Heat the oil in a deep-fryer or large pan until it reaches 180°C/350°F. Cook the wontons in the hot oil in small batches for around a minute on either side. The wontons are cooked when they float up and the skins have turned golden brown. Drain the excess oil on paper towels.

To make dipping sauce, sweeten the mayonnaise with the condensed milk and stir in the diced mango. Serve the wontons hot with the mango dipping sauce.

CRISPY CHICKEN WONTONS

Deep-frying these dumplings until they are crisp transforms them into an appetizing snack. When served with the dipping sauce, they go perfectly with pre-dinner drinks. Chinese black rice vinegar is available from Asian stores.

1 chicken breast fillet (approx. 140 g/5 oz.), finely minced

4 tbsp finely chopped fresh Chinese chives

pinch of ground Sichuan pepper

1 tsp light soy sauce

½ tsp sesame oil

16 wonton wrappers

sunflower or vegetable oil, for deep frying

salt and black pepper

DIPPING SAUCE

2 tbsp Chinese black rice vinegar

1 tsp sugar

1 garlic clove, finely chopped

½ red chilli/chile, finely chopped (optional)

MAKES 16

Thoroughly mix together the minced chicken, Chinese chives, Sichuan pepper, soy sauce and sesame oil. Season well with salt and pepper.

Mix together the ingredients for the dipping sauce and set aside.

Take a wonton wrapper and place a teaspoon of the chicken mixture in the centre of the wrapper. Brush the edges with a little cold water and bring the wrapper together over the chicken to form a parcel, pressing together well to seal properly. Set aside. Repeat the process until all 16 wrappers have been filled.

Heat the oil in a large saucepan or deep-fryer until very hot. Add four of the wontons and fry for a few minutes, until golden brown on both sides, turning over halfway through to ensure even browning. Remove with a slotted spoon and drain on paper towels. Repeat the process with the remaining wontons.

Serve at once with the dipping sauce.

VEGETARIAN SPRING ROLLS

15 g/⅔ cup dried black cloud ear fungus

25 g/1 oz. cellophane/glass noodles

75 g/3 oz. carrots

50 g/a small handful of mangetout/snow peas

1 tbsp vegetable oil

1 tsp freshly grated ginger

25 g/scant ½ cup spinach, torn

1 tbsp light or dark soy sauce

1 tbsp oyster sauce

a pinch of freshly ground black pepper

16 large spring roll wrappers

1–2 eggs, lightly beaten

sweet chilli/chile sauce, to serve

a baking sheet lined with baking parchment

SERVES 4

These are the quintessential Chinese takeaway/takeout appetizer choice. The perfectly crisp spring rolls can be filled with a multitude of vegetables and fish or meat, but here we have stuck to a vegetarian version. The fresh filling contrasts beautifully with the deep-fried wrappers for the perfect small snack.

Put the mushrooms in a large mixing bowl, cover with boiling water and soak for 20 minutes until softened. Drain well, pat dry with paper towels and slice thinly, discarding any tough stalks. Set aside.

Meanwhile put the noodles in a bowl, cover with boiling water and soak for 30 minutes until softened. Drain the noodles and pat dry with paper towels. Using scissors, cut the noodles into 5-cm/2-inch lengths and set aside.

Cut the carrots into 5-cm/2-inch batons and the mangetout into similar-sized shreds.

Heat the oil in a wok or large frying pan/skillet and stir-fry the ginger for a few seconds before adding the carrots and mangetout. Stir-fry for 2 minutes before adding the mushrooms, spinach, soy sauce, oyster sauce and black pepper. Stir well and remove the pan from the heat. Stir in the noodles and set aside to cool completely.

Working one wrapper at a time, trim each to 12 x 18 cm/ 4¾ x 7 inches, lay out flat and brush the top with beaten egg. Place a tablespoon of the cooled filling in a log shape along one edge of the wrapper. Roll over once, then fold the ends in and over the roll. Continue to roll up tightly to form a sealed parcel.

Preheat the oven to 110°C/225°F/Gas ¼, or the lowest heat setting.

Pour vegetable oil into a wok or large pan to reach about 5 cm/ 2 inches up the side and set over a medium–high heat. Heat until a cube of bread dropped into the oil crisps in 30 seconds. Deep-fry the rolls a few at a time for about 1–2 minutes until crisp and golden. Drain on paper towels and transfer the rolls to the prepared baking sheet.

Turn off the oven and set in the still-warm oven while you cook the remaining rolls in the same way.

Serve the spring rolls hot with sweet chilli sauce.

CHINESE EGG ROLLS

There is something so satisfying about an egg roll. Maybe it's the crunch; maybe it's the texture; maybe it's something about how pork and cabbage come together so well when hugged between egg roll wrappers and deep-fried. Whatever it is, they're delicious!

3 tbsp olive oil

1 tsp sea salt

1 tsp black pepper

1 tsp ground ginger

1 tsp garlic powder

450 g/1 lb. pork shoulder

2 tbsp plain/all-purpose flour

2 tbsp water

120 g/2 cups cabbage, shredded

1 carrot, shredded

8 x 18-cm/7-inch square egg roll wrappers

1 litre/4 cups groundnut/peanut oil, for frying

2 tbsp toasted sesame seeds (optional)

SWEET & SOUR DIPPING SAUCE

1 tbsp soy sauce

1 tbsp water

3½ tbsp caster/superfine sugar

3½ tbsp white vinegar

zest of 1 unwaxed orange

meat thermometer

MAKES 8

Preheat the oven to 180°C/350°F/Gas 4.

Rub the oil, salt, ground black pepper, ginger and garlic powder onto the pork shoulder.

Set the meat on a rack set into a roasting pan. Roast for 20 minutes, and then reduce the heat to 160°C/325°F/Gas 3. Continue to cook until a meat thermometer inserted into the shoulder reads 85°C/185°F, about 1–2 hours. Remove the pork from the oven and let stand until cool enough to handle, about 30 minutes. Shred the pork.

Combine the flour and water in a bowl until they form a paste. In a separate bowl combine the cabbage, carrot and shredded pork and mix them together.

Lay out one egg roll wrapper with a corner pointed toward you.

Place about 20 g/⅓ cup of the cabbage, carrot and shredded pork mixture onto the wrapper and fold the corner up over the mixture.

Fold the left and right corners toward the centre and continue to roll. Brush a bit of the flour paste on the final corner to help seal.

In a large frying pan/skillet, heat the groundnut oil to about 190°C/375°F. Place the egg rolls into the heated oil and fry, turning occasionally, until golden brown. Remove from oil and drain on paper towels. Put on a serving plate and top with toasted sesame seeds, if desired.

To make the sweet and sour sauce, mix all the ingredients together in a mixing bowl. Transfer to a small saucepan and bring to the boil, then remove from the heat. Pour the sauce into a small bowl ready to dip the egg rolls into.

NOODLE-WRAPPED PRAWNS
WITH SWEET CHILLI SAUCE

A great use of both noodles and prawns/shrimp make these a lovely canapé or finger food that looks quite striking on a platter for a party.

- 100 g/3½ oz. dried thin egg noodles
- 24 large prawns/shrimp, peeled and deveined
- vegetable oil, for deep frying

SWEET CHILLI SAUCE

- 2 heads of garlic, cloves peeled
- ¼ tsp salt
- 6 long red chillies/chiles, deseeded
- 4 tbsp caster/granulated sugar
- 2 tbsp rice wine vinegar
- 1 tsp light soy sauce

a baking sheet lined with baking parchment

SERVES 4

Start by making the sauce. Put all the ingredients in a saucepan set over a medium heat and bring to the boil, stirring to dissolve the sugar. Reduce the heat, cover and simmer gently for about 15 minutes until the garlic is tender. Cool slightly, then transfer the mixture to a food processor. Blend until smooth and return the mixture to the pan. Simmer uncovered for 10–15 minutes until the sauce is thick and glossy. Remove from the heat and set aside to cool.

Put the noodles in a bowl, cover with boiling water and soak for 20 minutes until softened. Drain the noodles and pat dry with paper towels. Wrap 8–10 noodles around each prawn and then set aside.

Preheat the oven to 110°C/225°F/Gas ¼ (or to the lowest setting).

Pour vegetable oil into a wok or large saucepan to reach about 5 cm/2 inches up the side and set over a medium-high heat. Heat until a cube of bread dropped into the oil crisps in about 30 seconds. Deep-fry the wrapped prawns in batches for about 2–3 minutes until the noodles are crisp and prawns are cooked.

Turn off the oven and set in the still-warm oven while you cook the remaining prawns in the same way.

Serve with the sweet chilli sauce.

BARBECUE PORK PUFFS

Light, flaky pastry is here the yin to the yang of the dark and rich barbecue pork that has been slow-cooked for maximum flavour.

1 pack of shop-bought puff pastry dough

1 tbsp sunflower oil

1 shallot, chopped

2 tbsp dry sherry

225 g/8 oz. pork loin, diced

1 tsp crushed/minced garlic

2 tbsp honey

2 tbsp hoisin sauce

1 tsp Chinese five-spice powder

1 tbsp soy sauce

1 egg, beaten

black sesame seeds, to garnish

a large baking sheet, greased

MAKES ABOUT 12

For the filling, heat the oil in a flameproof casserole dish and add the chopped shallot. Cook until softened and lightly caramelized, about 5–7 minutes. Pour in the sherry and let the alcohol cook out. Lower the heat to medium and add in the diced pork. Cook, stirring, for an extra 2 minutes or until lightly browned.

Meanwhile, mix the garlic, honey, hoisin sauce, five-spice powder and soy sauce in a bowl with 2 tablespoons of water. Add this to the pork and shallot, stirring well. Cover and cook for 1 hour over a low heat until the sauce has thickened and the pork is soft. Check occasionally during cooking to ensure the sauce does not dry out. Add a little extra water if necessary.

Preheat the oven to 200°C/400°F/Gas 6. Finely chop the pork once it is cool, ready for filling the pastry.

Divide the pastry in half. Roll each half into about six 10 x 6-cm/ 4 x 2½-inch rectangles, then cut each in half widthways. Put a small tablespoon of filling on one half, brush the edges with beaten egg and position a second piece of pastry on top to make about 12 puffs. Use a fork to make indentations and to tightly seal the edges.

Place the parcels on the greased baking sheet, brush the tops with beaten egg and sprinkle with black sesame seeds to garnish.

Bake in the preheated oven for 20–25 minutes, or until golden brown. Serve warm.

BEEF BULGOGI PUFFS

1 pack of shop-bought puff pastry dough

4 spring onions/scallions finely chopped

½ onion, finely chopped

¼ pineapple (pear or kiwi will also work), finely chopped

1 tbsp dark soy sauce

1 tbsp sugar

1 tsp sesame oil

freshly ground black pepper

2 garlic cloves, crushed/minced

1 tbsp freshly squeezed lemon juice

150 g/5¼ oz. sirloin steak, sliced into bite-size strips

1 egg, beaten

white sesame seeds, to garnish

chilli/chile sauce, for dipping

a griddle/grill pan, lightly greased

a large baking sheet, greased

MAKES ABOUT 12

Using a good cut of beef for the filling here is key; you want the meat to be almost as soft as the flaky pastry on the outside.

Stir together the filling ingredients, apart from the meat, in a large bowl to form a marinade paste, adding a little water to loosen if necessary. Mix the beef strips with the paste, making sure that each strip is well coated. Leave in the fridge to marinate for at least 30 minutes and up to 2 hours; left longer than this the beef may become too salty.

Heat a griddle/grill pan over a medium-high heat, add the beef strips and juices to the pan and cook until the meat is browned around the edges and cooked to your liking, around 3–7 minutes. Remove from the pan and leave to cool.

Preheat the oven to 200°C/400°F/Gas 6.

Divide the pastry into about 12 portions. Roll each portion into a 10 cm/4 inch square. Put a tablespoon of filling in the middle of one square and brush the edges with a little beaten egg. Fold the pastry in half diagonally to create a triangle. Seal the edges then tuck the seams underneath to create a smooth finish on top. Repeat with the remaining dough and filling.

Place the puffs on the greased baking sheet, brush with beaten egg, sprinkle with sesame seeds and bake for about 20–25 minutes until golden brown. Serve with chilli sauce for dipping.

DUCK CONFIT PUFFS

pictured on page 64

Juicy duck confit with the flavour of aromatic crispy duck is a delectable treat that works perfectly in these bite-sized little pastry puffs.

1 pack of shop-bought puff pastry dough

2 duck legs

60 g/¼ cup sea salt flakes, plus extra for serving

1 tbsp freshly ground black pepper

1 garlic clove, crushed/minced

2 tbsp Chinese five-spice powder

5 star anise

1 cinnamon stick

2 cloves

500 g/1 lb. duck fat

2 spring onions/scallions, chopped

2 tbsp hoisin sauce

1 egg, beaten

white sesame seeds, to garnish

a small round pastry cutter

MAKES ABOUT 12

Rub the duck legs with the sea salt flakes, black pepper, crushed garlic clove, five-spice powder, star anise, cinnamon stick and cloves. Pack the duck and these ingredients tightly into a dish, skin-side down. Cover the dish with cling film/plastic wrap and leave to marinate in the fridge for 24 hours.

Preheat the oven to 150°C/300°F/Gas 2.

Scrape the marinade off the duck pieces. Heat the duck fat in an ovenproof dish until melted, then add the duck legs, ensuring they are completely submerged.

Bake the duck in the preheated oven for 3½ hours, or until the meat is very tender when pierced with a skewer and the fat in the skin is rendered. Once cooked, remove the duck from the fat and allow to cool uncovered. Shred finely and mix with the chopped spring onions and hoisin sauce.

Roll out the puff pastry dough into a large rectangle. Using a small round pastry cutter, stamp out about 24 rounds. Put a spoonful of filling on one half, brush the edges with beaten egg and position a second piece of pastry on top. Use a fork to make indentations around the edge to tightly seal. Brush the tops with beaten egg and sprinkle with white sesame seeds. Bake in the preheated oven for about 20–25 minutes until golden brown.

MIXED MUSHROOM PUFFS

Button, shiitake and oyster mushrooms are used to fill these dumplings, but you don't have to stick to this mixture exactly. The shiitake mushrooms bring a nice umami-like depth of flavour, so do use these if you can.

1 pack of shop-bought puff pastry dough

2 shallots, chopped

1 garlic clove, chopped

1 tsp minced fresh ginger

4 button mushrooms, sliced

4 shiitake mushrooms, sliced

4 oyster mushrooms, sliced

2 spring onions/scallions, sliced

salt and black pepper

1 egg, beaten

black sesame seeds, to garnish

a large baking sheet, greased

MAKES ABOUT 12

Preheat the oven to 200°C/400°F/Gas 6.

In a small frying pan/skillet, cook the shallots over a medium heat for a few minutes until fragrant. Add the garlic and ginger and stir-fry together for a couple of minutes. Add the sliced mushrooms, spring onions and some salt and pepper. Fry until the mushrooms are cooked and the mixture is dry. Set aside to cool.

Divide the pastry into about 12 portions. Roll each portion into a rectangle 10 x 6 cm/4 x 2½ inches. Put a small tablespoon of filling on one side of a skin, brush the edges with beaten egg and fold in half to enclose the filling. Use a fork to make indentations and tightly seal the edges. Repeat with the rest of the dough and filling.

Place the parcels on the greased baking sheet, brush the tops with beaten egg and sprinkle with black sesame seeds to garnish. Bake in the preheated oven for about 20–25 minutes or until golden brown. Serve warm.

WRAPPED & ROLLED

OTHER FILLED PARCELS & ROLLS

VIETNAMESE VEGETABLE SUMMER ROLLS

Light and fresh, rice papers make a good gluten-free option for wheat-intolerant dim sum lovers. The peanut butter, hoisin and lime juice dipping sauce adds a touch of richness and piquancy to the dish, for those who want it.

80 g/1¼ cup vermicelli rice noodles

14 edible rice papers

14 Bibb or other soft lettuce leaves

100 g/1¾ cups beansprouts

14 thin peeled carrot batons

14 thin cucumber batons

2 handfuls fresh coriander/cilantro leaves, roughly chopped

14 fresh mint leaves, roughly chopped

1 red chilli/chile, sliced

DIPPING SAUCE

4 tbsp hoisin sauce

4 tbsp peanut butter

lime juice to taste

MAKES 14

Prepare the dipping sauce by mixing together all the ingredients in a small bowl. Cover and refrigerate until needed.

Cook the vermicelli according to instructions on the packet. Drain and set aside.

Soften the rice papers. Fill a large bowl with warm water. Carefully and slowly dip the rice papers in one by one. Leave each one for about 20 seconds until totally soft. Lay the rice papers out on a dry cloth as you finish.

On top of each rice paper, arrange a lettuce leaf (trimmed to size if needed) a small handful of vermicelli and a small handful of beansprouts. Add carrot, cucumber, herbs and chilli, always keeping about 5 cm/2 inches of wrapper uncovered on each side of the filling.

Fold the uncovered sides inwards, then tightly roll the rice paper into a sausage shape around the filling. Repeat with the remaining ingredients.

Serve the rolls chilled with the dipping sauce to accompany.

SMOKED DUCK SUMMER ROLLS

100 g/3½ oz. rice vermicelli noodles

2 tsp fish sauce

2 tsp lime juice

2 tsp caster/granulated sugar

8 x 20-cm/8-inch dried rice paper wrappers

100 g/3½ oz. smoked duck breast

100 g/3 cups thinly sliced lettuce

1 carrot, peeled and cut into thin batons

½ cucumber, deseeded and cut into matchsticks

20 fresh Thai basil leaves

HOISIN & PEANUT DIPPING SAUCE

2 tbsp hoisin sauce

1 tbsp smooth peanut butter

1 tbsp warm water

2 tsp freshly squeezed lime juice

1 tsp dark soy sauce

¼ tsp caster/granulated sugar

SERVES 4

Called 'summer rolls' and typically served in summer months due to their refreshing nature, these can have many different fillings. This recipe uses thin slices of smoked duck breast (available from specialist food stores), but if you can't find smoked duck you could use smoked salmon or smoked trout instead.

Put the noodles in a bowl, cover with boiling water and soak for 30 minutes until softened. Drain the noodles, pat dry and transfer to a large mixing bowl. Whisk the fish sauce, lime juice and sugar together until the sugar is dissolved and pour over the noodles. Toss well and set aside.

Next make the dipping sauce. Put all the ingredients in a small saucepan set over a low heat. Heat gently, stirring until the peanut butter is softened and the sauce smooth. Remove from the heat and set aside to cool.

Working one at a time, dip the rice paper wrappers into a bowl of warm water for about a minute until softened and then pat dry on paper towels. Lay each wrapper out flat and top with a few noodles, the smoked duck slices, shredded lettuce, carrot, cucumber and basil leaves. Fold the ends of the rice paper over the filling and then roll up tightly to form parcels.

Serve with the dipping sauce.

STEAMED FLAT RICE NOODLE & ASPARAGUS ROLLS

Flat rice noodle rolls are a classic on dim sum menus, and they are very easily made at home to add to your own Asian spreads.

70 g/generous ½ cup rice flour

10 g/1 tbsp plus 1 tsp tapioca starch

20 g/3 tbsp plus 1 tsp cornflour/cornstarch

1 tbsp sunflower or vegetable oil

12 asparagus spears, peeled

1 tbsp black sesame seeds, to garnish

SWEET SOY SAUCE

2 tsp clear honey or sugar

2 tbsp light soy sauce

2 tsp sesame oil

MAKES 18

Put the rice flour, tapioca starch and cornflour into a bowl and add 360 ml/1½ cups water. Whisk until evenly mixed.

Put a heatproof dish into the steamer basket and heat it over rapidly boiling water. Using either dish tongs or heatproof gloves, carefully remove the hot heatproof dish from the steamer basket. Brush the base of the dish with the oil.

Give the rice flour mixture a quick stir, then use a ladle to scoop a thin layer of mixture into the hot dish, tilting the dish so the mixture spreads evenly. Place two asparagus spears along the middle. Put the dish back into the steamer basket and steam for about 40 seconds over a high heat, or until you see bubbles forming on the flat noodles (it needs to be steaming over rapidly boiling water, otherwise it may take a little longer).

Carefully remove the dish from the basket. Using a flat scraper, gently roll the flat noodle with the asparagus spears in the centre. Cut the noodle roll into three portions.

Repeat the process another five times with the remaining mixture and asparagus spears.

To make the sauce, heat 2 tablespoons water in a small pan and add the honey (or sugar), soy sauce and sesame oil. Stir until dissolved.

Serve the rice noodle rolls with the sauce for diners to add to their liking. Garnish with black sesame seeds.

VEGAN TEMAKI ROLLS WITH SEED PÂTÉ

This hand-rolled sushi is really easy to make. Temakis are a great choice for parties since they are best rolled directly at the table, just before eating, and everybody can join in, which leaves you with less work. Prepare and serve all ingredients in the middle of the table and let the fun begin!

FERMENTED SEED PÂTÉ

240 g/2 cups pumpkin seeds

840 ml/3½ cups water, for soaking

50 ml/scant ¼ cup olive oil

60 ml/¼ cup water

1 garlic clove

¼ tsp turmeric powder

1 tbsp nutritional yeast (optional)

3 tsp vegan rice or barley miso

2 tsp lemon juice

¼ tsp salt

black pepper

MAKES 250 G/ 2½ CUPS

TEMAKI ROLLS

2 medium carrots (around 100 g/3½ oz. total weight)

1 ripe avocado (around 190 g/6½ oz. in weight)

2 handfuls rocket/ arugula or 50 g/1 cup alfalfa sprouts, plus extra to serve

3 spring onions/ scallions

6 sheets of nori seaweed

2 cups sauerkraut or other fermented vegetables, plus extra to serve

soy sauce, to serve

MAKES 12

First make the pâté. Soak the pumpkin seeds in the water for soaking for about 2–3 days, until slightly fermented, without changing the soaking water. Discard the soaking water and rinse them thoroughly under running water. Drain well. Place in a high-speed blender jug/pitcher, together with the remaining ingredients. Blend until smooth, using a tamper tool to push down the ingredients. If you don't own a high-speed blender, the pâté will probably turn out chunkier in a less powerful blender, and more water will need to be added, resulting in a somewhat runnier consistency.

Let sit in the fridge for another day; the flavours really develop in this final stage of setting. There will be some leftovers, but you can store these in the fridge and use within a week.

Wash and julienne the carrots. Peel the avocado, slice in half, discard the stone

and cut both halves in strips. Wash the rocket or sprouts and pat dry. Take only the green parts of the spring onions, wash them well and cut into 10-cm/4-inch pieces. Cut each nori sheet in half with scissors.

Make sure your hands are dry before starting. Place a piece of nori (shiny side down) in the palm of your hand and add 1½ tablespoons pumpkin seed pâté. Spread it gently on the left third of the nori sheet.

Place your chosen fillings diagonally over the pate. Do not overfill; a couple of carrot matchsticks, 1 slice of avocado, 1 tablespoon of sauerkraut and some greens are more than enough. Fold the bottom left corner of the nori over and begin rolling into a cone shape. Wet the edge with a little water and seal. Continue until all the nori is used.

Serve the temaki rolls with more fermented vegetables, condiments, some soy sauce and leftover greens.

BEEF BULGOGI & RICE NOODLE WRAPS

The Korean word bulgogi means 'fire meat' and refers to marinated and grilled meats, usually beef. Here it is stir-fried and combined with shiitake mushrooms and Korean sweet potato noodles, wrapped in lettuce leaves and topped with kimchi and ssamjang.

500 g/1 lb. beef rib-eye steak
2 tbsp light or dark soy sauce
2 tbsp soft brown sugar
1 Asian shallot, finely chopped
1 garlic clove, crushed
2 tsp sesame oil, plus extra for dressing
½ tsp Chinese five-spice powder
125 g/4 oz. spiralized sweet potato noodles
2 tbsp peanut oil
125 g/4 oz. shiitake mushrooms, trimmed and cut into quarters
4 tbsp kimchi
Ssamjang (see page 115, or buy ready-made), to serve

SERVES 4

Begin by preparing the beef. Thinly slice the steak and arrange in a single layer in a wide, shallow dish. Combine the soy sauce, sugar, shallot, garlic, sesame oil and Chinese five-spice powder, and pour over the beef. Set aside to marinate for at least 1 hour.

Plunge the sweet potato noodles into a pan of boiling water and cook for 4–5 minutes until al dente. Drain, refresh under cold water and drain again. Shake the noodles dry and dress with a little sesame oil to prevent them from sticking together. Set aside.

Heat the oil in a wok or large frying pan/skillet set over a medium heat until it starts to shimmer. Add the beef in batches and stir-fry for 2–3 minutes until golden. Remove with a slotted spoon. Add the mushrooms and any remaining marinade and stir-fry for 1 minute. Return the beef to the pan along with the noodles and stir-fry for 1 minute, until everything is heated through.

Serve with lettuce leaves, kimchi and ssamjang. Wrap, roll and eat.

BOK CHOY ROLLS WITH SPICY CHICKEN

100 g/½ cup plus 1 tbsp long-grain rice

36 large Chinese leaves, such as large pak choi/bok choy, choi sum or Chinese cabbage, about 500 g/1 lb. 2 oz.

350 g/12 oz. skinless, boneless chicken breast, minced/ground

6 spring onions/scallions, chopped

2 garlic cloves, crushed/minced

4-cm/1½-inch piece fresh ginger, peeled and grated

2 green chillies/chiles, deseeded and finely chopped

2 tsp Chinese five-spice powder

2 tbsp hoisin or yellow bean sauce

150 g/1 cup canned water chestnuts, drained and chopped

salt

plum sauce, to serve

MAKES 36

In Eastern Europe, meat and rice wrapped in cabbage is very popular. The idea lends itself very well to Chinese ingredients, making perfect dim sum. There are many popular vegetables from the cabbage family in Chinese cuisine – any are suitable here, as long as the leaves are big enough.

Boil the rice in salted water for 10 minutes, then drain.

Separate the leaves of the pak choi, choi sum or cabbage – each should be at least 12.5 x 7.5 cm/5 x 3 inches big. Blanch in a saucepan of boiling water, then refresh in cold water. Set aside.

Put the chicken, spring onions, garlic, ginger, chillies, Chinese five-spice, hoisin or yellow bean sauce and water chestnuts in a bowl and mix well.

Put a tablespoon of the mixture in the centre of each leaf and roll up. Place in the steamer basket lined with parchment paper (cook in batches, if necessary). Steam over boiling water for 10 minutes, then serve with plum sauce.

PEKING-STYLE DUCK PANCAKE WRAPS

4 duck breasts, 150 g/ 5¼ oz. each

4 tbsp dark soy sauce

1 tbsp clear honey

2 tsp Chinese five-spice powder

1 tbsp groundnut/peanut oil

salt

TO SERVE

1 cucumber

24 Chinese Peking duck pancakes

125 ml/½ cup hoisin sauce

6 spring onions/scallions, halved lengthways and crossways

sesame seeds

24 squares of parchment paper, 12-cm/5-inch square

MAKES 24

Cooking traditional Peking duck is a time-consuming process involving drying, boiling and basting, not to mention the actual cooking! A much easier option is buying a ready prepared duck. Another simple solution is to use just the duck breast, which gives a succulent, simple result. These wraps always go down well at parties. The paper wrappers keep them moist and stop them sticking together if you prepare them in advance. Peking duck pancakes are sold by Chinese grocers – find them in the freezer or chiller cabinet.

Score the duck fat diagonally at 5-mm/¼-in. intervals and rub in about 1 tablespoon salt. Mix the soy sauce, honey and Chinese five-spice in a flat glass or ceramic dish. Put the duck breasts, skin-side up, in the marinade, moving them about so the flesh is coated. Cover and set aside in the fridge to marinate for at least 2 hours.

Remove the duck from the marinade and pat dry with paper towels.

Heat the oil in a frying pan/skillet over a medium heat, add the duck breasts, skin-side down, and cook for 8 minutes. Pour off the fat from the pan, then turn the breasts and cook the other side for 4 minutes. Remove from the pan and let cool.

Slice each duck breast diagonally into 12 strips.

Quarter the cucumber lengthways, then scoop out and discard the seeds. Slice each quarter in six lengthways and then in half crossways. You should have 48 pieces.

Place the pancakes in the steamer basket lined with parchment paper and steam over boiling water for 5 minutes.

When filling, work on 3–4 pancakes at a time and keep the others covered with a damp kitchen cloth so they don't dry out. Spread a teaspoon of hoisin sauce on each pancake, then add a couple of pieces of duck, a few strips of cucumber, a piece of spring onion and some sesame seeds. Fold up the bottom, then the sides. Wrap the pieces of parchment paper around the pancakes in the same way, then cover with a cloth until ready to serve.

SALMON & ASIAN PESTO PARCELS

These delicate parcels with a hint of green herb and a pink cloud of salmon showing through translucent rice paper wrappers are a modern update on a Chinese classic. Serving with Asian pesto also gives them a new twist.

650 g/1 lb. 7 oz. skinless salmon fillet

20 rice paper wrappers

a small bunch of fresh coriander/cilantro, leaves only

1 tbsp groundnut/peanut oil

dipping sauce of your choice, to serve

ASIAN PESTO

4 garlic cloves, crushed/minced

60 g/½ cup cashew nuts, chopped

a large bunch of coriander/cilantro, leaves only

a large bunch of Thai basil (or ordinary basil), leaves only

80 ml/⅓ cup groundnut/peanut oil

MAKES 20

To make the pesto, put all the ingredients in a small food processor and grind to a fairly smooth paste. Alternatively, use a mortar and pestle.

Cut the salmon into 20 even pieces, about 5-cm/2-inches square.

Dip a rice paper wrapper in warm water to soften, put a coriander leaf in the centre, then top with a piece of salmon and a teaspoon of pesto. Fold in the sides to form a neat square (trim the edges if the wrapper is too big). The damp wrappers will stick closed. Repeat with the remaining wrappers and fillings.

Heat the oil in a frying pan/skillet and cook the parcels, in batches, sealed-side down, for 3 minutes until brown.

Transfer them to the steamer basket, leaving space between them. Steam over boiling water for 4–6 minutes until the salmon is cooked.

Serve on their own or with a dipping sauce of your choice.

MALAYSIAN FISH PARCELS

600 g/1 lb. 5 oz. firm boneless fish, such as salmon, mackerel or cod

4 eggs

3 makrut lime leaves, central stems removed and remainder thinly sliced

250 ml/1 cup coconut cream

banana leaves, for wrapping (optional)

salt

CHILLI/CHILE PASTE

5 dried chillies/chiles, soaked in boiling water for 15 minutes

5 red bird's eye chillies/chiles, chopped

5 Thai pink shallots or 1 regular

2 garlic cloves, crushed/minced

2 stalks lemongrass, trimmed, peeled and thinly sliced

2.5-cm/1-inch piece fresh ginger, peeled and sliced

1 tbsp fish sauce

1 tsp ground turmeric

MAKES 2

Banana leaves are the traditional wraps for this Malaysian-inspired dish, but you could also use foil or even greaseproof paper. If you want something slightly less fiery, use fewer chillies/chiles.

Cut the fish into 5 x 2.5-cm/2 x 1-inch pieces, sprinkle with 1 teaspoon salt and set aside for 15 minutes.

To make the chilli paste, drain the soaked chillies and put into a small blender. Add the bird's eye chillies, shallots, garlic, lemongrass, ginger, fish sauce and turmeric and blend well. Alternatively, use a mortar and pestle.

Put the eggs into a bowl and beat lightly with a fork. Add the chilli paste and lime leaves and stir well. Stir in the coconut cream and 1 teaspoon salt.

Wash and dry the banana leaves, if using (or use foil instead). Warm them over an open flame for a few seconds until softened, then cut into pieces about 17.5 x 15 cm/7 x 6 inches.

Put a piece of fish in the centre of each piece of leaf. Bring the two long sides together, then fold one of the short sides so the middle meets the two long edges. Fold the wings back and keep together (you could use a paperclip or plastic clothes peg/clothes pin). Add about 2 tablespoons of the egg mixture to the parcel and fold the other end in the same way. Fasten with a long cocktail stick/toothpick or bamboo skewer. You can also trim the top with scissors to make a neat parcel, if you like. Place in the steamer basket.

Steam over boiling water for 20 minutes, then serve with a selection of other Asian dishes.

STEAMED TOFU SKIN WITH WILD MUSHROOM FILLING

Tofu/beancurd skins soak up the rich flavours of the mushrooms and gochujang as they soften in the steamer. Dried tofu skins will need to be soaked according to the packet instructions before use.

- 100 g/3½ oz. wood ear/cloud ear mushrooms, soaked in water for 24 hours
- 150 g/5¼ oz. shiitake mushrooms
- 150 g/5¼ oz. king oyster mushrooms
- 200 g/7 oz. enoki mushrooms
- 2 carrots
- 1 yellow (bell) pepper
- 100 g/3½ oz. Chinese chives
- 3 tbsp vegetable or sunflower oil
- 1 tbsp chopped garlic
- 2 tsp ground ginger
- 1 tbsp gochujang (Korean chilli/chile paste)
- 2 tbsp light soy sauce
- 8 sheets soft tofu/beancurd skin, 10-cm/4-inch square
- salt and black pepper

MAKES 8

Drain the wood ear mushrooms, then slice them thinly along with the other mushrooms. Julienne the carrots, (bell) pepper and Chinese chives into thin strips about 6 cm/2½ inch long.

Heat the oil in a frying pan/skillet, add the mushrooms and fry until they are softened. Add the garlic and ginger and continue to fry until fragrant. Add the julienned vegetables and give the pan a quick toss, then add the gochujang, soy sauce and 250 ml/1 cup water. Bring it to a simmer and cook for a few minutes, then season with salt and pepper to taste and remove from the heat. Allow the mixture to cool.

Strain the filling through a fine-mesh sieve/strainer, reserving the strained sauce, then divide the filling into eight portions.

Arrange the tofu/beancurd skins on the work surface and add a portion of filling to each, placing it at the base of the sheet. Roll each sheet around the filling, then place the filled rolls in a heatproof dish. Pour over the reserved sauce and place the dish into the steamer basket.

Steam over boiling water for 10 minutes until the tofu skin has softened. Allow to cool a little before serving with the sauce from the base of the dish.

LOTUS LEAF RICE DUMPLINGS

The lotus is considered a sacred plant in Chinese culture, the fruit of which is delicious but hard to find. More prevalent are the giant strong-textured leaves, perfect for holding a filling, but still pleasant to eat.

370 g/2 cups sweet glutinous/sticky rice

4 dried lotus leaves

½ tsp salt

1 tsp sesame oil

1 chicken breast, finely chopped

1 tbsp cornflour/cornstarch

2 tsp vegetable oil

4 shiitake mushrooms, sliced

1 leek, sliced

1 Chinese sausage (marinated and smoked pork sausage found in Chinese markets), thinly sliced

2 tsp oyster sauce

2 tsp soy sauce

1 tbsp Shaoxing rice wine

2 tbsp caster/superfine sugar

bamboo steamer, lined with parchment paper

rice cooker

MAKES 8

Rinse and drain the rice, then soak in 600 ml/2½ cups water for 2 hours.

Meanwhile, cut each folded lotus leaf in half lengthways. Submerge the leaves in hot water and leave to soak for 30 minutes, pressing down if they float up. Trim the leaves with kitchen scissors/shears until they are a similar size and trim off the hard stalk end.

Drain the rice thoroughly. In the bowl of a rice cooker, place the rice, salt, sesame oil and 250 ml/1 cup water. Cook following the packet instructions.

Mix the chopped chicken with the cornflour. Put the oil in a large frying pan/skillet over a high heat and fry the chicken for 3 minutes. Add the mushrooms, sliced leek and sausage and cook, stirring for a further few minutes. Lower the heat and add the oyster sauce, soy sauce, Shaoxing rice wine and caster sugar. Stir-fry until chicken is cooked and the vegetables are tender. Set aside to cool.

Divide the cooked rice into 8 portions. With wet fingertips, divide each portion of rice in half. Shape 8 half-portions into rectangles in the centre of each lotus leaf half. Put 1 tablespoon of chicken mixture on top and spread evenly. Top the meat with the other halves of rice to cover them completely.

Fold the bottom of the leaves up over the rice. Fold in the left and right sides, and then roll each leaf away from you towards the curved edge to make a rectangular packet. Place the dumplings seam-side down on the bamboo steamer. Steam over boiling water for about 45 minutes, or until heated through. Serve warm.

STEAMED CABBAGE LEAF SPRING ROLLS
WITH MIXED VEG FILLING *pictured on page 84*

Savoy cabbage rolls are found across the globe. Here are another variation on cabbage rolls stuffed with Asian veggies and flavourings.

2 carrots

300 g/10½ oz. tung ho leaves (*Chrysanthemum coronarium*)

200 g/7 oz. enoki mushrooms

200 g/7 oz. baby corn

100 g/3½ oz. fresh lotus roots

200 g/7 oz. rice vermicelli, soaked in water for 2 hours

1 tbsp chopped garlic

2 tsp grated fresh ginger

2 tbsp olive oil, plus extra for brushing

3 tbsp sesame oil

2 tbsp soy sauce

2 tbsp fried shallots

8 Savoy cabbage leaves

salt and black pepper

MAKES 8

Julienne the carrots, tung ho leaves and enoki into 6-cm/ 2¼-inch lengths. Halve the baby corns lengthways. Slice the lotus roots thinly and halve them. Blanch all the veg quickly, then set aside.

Drain the rice vermicelli and place in the steamer basket. Steam the rice vermicelli for 5 minutes over boiling water until softened.

Put the chopped garlic and grated ginger in a small heatproof bowl. Heat the olive oil in a small pan and pour the hot oil over the bowl of garlic and ginger.

Put the blanched veg and noodles into a bowl and add the sesame oil, soy sauce and fried shallots. Pour in the ginger and garlic mixture and season to taste. Mix well and set aside to cool.

Blanch the Savoy cabbage leaves in boiling water to soften them, the pat them dry and allow to cool.

Arrange the cabbage leaves on the work surface and divide the vegetable and noodle mixture between the leaves. Fold the leaves in from the sides, then roll them into spring rolls. Brush the tops with olive oil. Put the spring rolls in a round heatproof dish, then place in the steamer basket. Steam for 10 minutes over boiling water, then serve.

RICE PARCELS

This is an easy banana leaf version of a more complicated traditional recipe using dried lotus leaves. You can also use a simple foil packet.

4 dried shiitake mushrooms

300 g/1⅓ cups plus 3 tbsp jasmine rice

3-cm/1½-inch piece fresh ginger, peeled and sliced

2 tbsp groundnut/peanut oil

8 slices smoked bacon, sliced crossways

2 eggs

8 pieces banana leaf or dried lotus leaf soaked in boiling water until supple, or foil, 20-cm/8-inch square

FLAVOUR MIXTURE

1 tbsp mirin

1 tbsp dark soy sauce

1 tbsp oyster sauce

pinch of sugar

1 tsp sesame oil

MAKES 8

Put the mushrooms into a bowl, cover with boiling water and let soak for 30 minutes. Drain, remove and discard the stems and thinly slice the caps.

To make the flavour mixture, put the mirin, soy sauce, oyster sauce, sugar and sesame oil into a bowl, mix well, then set aside.

Put the rice and ginger into a saucepan and add enough water to come one finger's joint above the top of the rice. Bring to the boil, cover and cook for 8 minutes until the rice is part-cooked. Drain and discard the slices of ginger.

Heat the oil in a wok, add the bacon and stir-fry until crisp. Remove and set aside.

Put the eggs into a bowl and beat with 1 tablespoon water. Reheat the bacon fat in the wok and swirl so the sides are well coated, adding a little oil if necessary. Add the beaten eggs and swirl to form a thin omelette. Cook until just set, then roll up the omelette, transfer to a plate and slice thinly.

Put the banana leaf, lotus leaf or foil squares onto a work surface, put 1–2 tablespoons of rice in the centre, then a share of all the other ingredients, including the flavour mixture. Fold up into square parcels, tie with string/twine or secure with cocktail sticks/toothpicks, and set in the steamer basket.

Steam for about 20 minutes, then serve, cutting a cross in the top of each packet just before serving, so the aromas escape across the table.

FINISHING TOUCHES

SAUCES, DRIZZLES, DIPS & GARNISHES

CHINESE & JAPANESE DIPPING SAUCES

The Chinese soy and vinegar version (opposite, top) is a perfect sauce for wontons, while the Japanese version (opposite, below right) is traditionally served in hot summer months with chilled noodles.

CHINESE

50 ml/¼ cup light soy sauce

2 tsp Chinese black vinegar

1 tsp caster/superfine sugar

1 tsp freshly grated root ginger

1 tsp sesame oil

¼ tsp chilli/chile oil

MAKES 75 ML/ SCANT ⅓ CUP

JAPANESE

200 ml/¾ cup dashi broth

3 tbsp Japanese soy sauce

3 tbsp mirin

½ tsp caster/superfine sugar

MAKES 300 ML/1¼ CUPS

sterilized glass jars with airtight lids

For each sauce, whisk all the ingredients together in a bowl, or, if you have a clean glass jar with a lid, put all the ingredients into the jar, screw on the lid and shake well.

Serve immediately or store in a glass jar with an airtight lid in the fridge. The Chinese sauce will keep for up to 5 days but you can store the Japanese sauce in the fridge until it is all used up.

VIETNAMESE YIN YANG LIME JUICE

Vietnamese cuisine is based on the yin and yang philosophy, where balance is integral to the flavour of a dish, as well as life. This (opposite, below left) is a great example of the principle.

1 tsp sea salt

1 tsp freshly ground black pepper

1 lime, cut into wedges

MAKES 75 ML/SCANT ⅓ CUP

Make separate piles of salt and pepper on opposite sides of the same dish. Squeeze the juice from the lime over each pile. Using a chopstick or small spoon, mix the salt with a little of the juice and then mix the pepper in the same way to make a black paste and a white paste.

Shape into a yin yang symbol and serve.

KOREAN DIPPING SAUCES

Korea is famed for its love of the condiment or side dish. Choganjang is the simplest of dipping sauces (opposite, top left), perfect with all noodle dishes. If you prefer your sauces spicy, try Cho-gochujang (opposite, top right) – you can increase the amount of chilli/chile paste you use to suit your personal tastes if liked. Ssamjang is a spicy fermented chilli/chile bean paste (opposite, bottom), which is often served with Korean BBQ, but also delicious stirred into Korean soups.

CHOGANJANG

2 tbsp dark soy sauce

1 tbsp brown rice vinegar

a pinch of sesame seeds, toasted

MAKES 45 ML/3 TABLESPOONS

Pour the soy sauce and vinegar into a small bowl and sprinkle with a few sesame seeds.

Use as required or store the soy and vinegar mixture without the sesame seeds in a sterilized glass bottle until ready to serve.

CHO-GOCHUJANG

1 tbsp sesame seeds

1–2 tsp gochujang (Korean chilli/chile paste)

2 tbsp rice wine vinegar

2 tbsp dark soy sauce

1 tbsp clear honey

2 tsp sesame oil

1 spring onion/scallion, trimmed and finely chopped

1 garlic clove, crushed

MAKES 150 ML/⅔ CUP

Dry-fry the sesame seeds in a small frying pan/skillet set over a medium heat until evenly toasted. Transfer to a spice grinder or pestle and mortar and grind to a rough paste.

Put the ground sesame seeds in a small bowl and stir in the gochujang, vinegar, soy sauce, honey and sesame oil until smooth, then add the spring onion/scallion and garlic and stir well. Serve immediately.

SSAMJANG

60 ml/4 tbsp doenjang (Korean fermented soy beans)

2 tsp gochujang (Korean chilli/chile paste)

1 spring onion/scallion, trimmed and finely chopped

1 small garlic clove, crushed

1 Asian shallot, finely chopped

2 tsp rice wine

2 tsp sesame oil

1 tsp clear honey

1 tsp sesame seeds, toasted

MAKES 150 ML/⅔ CUP

Put all the ingredients in a small bowl and use as required.

Alternatively, transfer to a plastic container, seal and store in the fridge for up to 3 days.

WAFU DRESSING

Literally translated as 'Japanese-style', wafu is a soy, vinegar and sesame dressing (opposite, top) to which other flavourings can be added. It is delicious drizzled over simple leaf salads or more complex noodle salads and is a great recipe to have in your culinary arsenal.

1 small shallot, very finely chopped

2 tbsp Japanese soy sauce

2 tbsp rice wine vinegar

2 tbsp dashi broth

2 tsp sesame oil

2 tsp caster/superfine sugar

1 tsp freshly grated ginger

½ tsp crushed garlic

sterilized glass jar with airtight lid

MAKES 150 ML/ ⅔ CUP

Put all the ingredients in a sterilized glass jar, screw the lid on tightly and shake well until amalgamated.

Use as required. The dressing will keep in the fridge for up to 5 days.

Tip: Dashi broth can be bought in concentrated form from Asian stores or online.

SZECHUAN CHILLI DRESSING

The perfect sauce (opposite, bottom) for dipping hot steamed and fried wontons into.

100 ml/⅓ cup sunflower oil

1–2 tsp dried red chilli/hot red pepper flakes

2 tbsp light soy sauce

1 tbsp black vinegar

2 tsp caster/superfine sugar

¼ tsp Szechuan peppercorns

MAKES 200 ML/ ¾ CUP

Heat the oil in a small saucepan set over a medium heat until it just starts to shimmer. Remove from the heat and stir in the chilli/hot red pepper flakes. Set aside for 30 minutes, then strain through a fine mesh sieve/strainer into a clean bowl. Stir in the remaining ingredients and serve as required.

Tip: If you are making this dressing ahead of time, omit the peppercorns and add just before serving.

NUOC CHAM *pictured on page 110, right*

A classic Vietnamese sauce served with everything from salads and soups to stir-fries. There are countless variations of this sauce but all are hot, salty, sweet and sour – flavours so beloved in South-east Asia. Feel free to add more chilli/chile if you enjoy a hotter flavour.

2 large red chillies/ chiles, chopped

2 red bird's eye chillies/chiles, deseeded and chopped

2 garlic cloves, crushed

4 tbsp grated palm sugar

4 tbsp Thai fish sauce

grated zest and juice of 4 limes

salt and pepper

MAKES ABOUT 100 ML/SCANT ½ CUP

Put the chillies, garlic and palm sugar in a pestle and mortar or food processor and pound or blend to form a paste. Transfer to a mixing bowl and whisk in the remaining ingredients.

Store in an airtight container in the fridge and use as required.

GREEN NAM JIM *pictured on page 110, left*

The Thai equivalent to nuoc cham. Nam jim is here made with green chillies/chiles for a striking contrast to the Vietnamese version, but red or green can be used, as desired.

2 green bird's eye chillies/ chiles, deseeded and roughly chopped

4 garlic cloves, chopped

a large pinch of salt

2 tbsp chopped fresh coriander/cilantro

4 tbsp grated palm sugar

4 tbsp fish sauce

4 tbsp lime juice

MAKES ABOUT 100 ML/SCANT ½ CUP

Put the chilli, garlic and salt in a pestle and mortar or food processor and pound or blend to form a paste. Transfer to a mixing bowl and stir in the coriander, palm sugar, fish sauce and lime juice, and stir until the sugar is dissolved.

Store in an airtight container in the fridge and use as required.

SAMBAL OLEK

This Malaysian chilli/chile sauce has a lovely depth of flavour to it with a hint of tamarind, which is very fragrant.

5 Asian shallots, chopped

25 g/scant ¼ cup chopped large red chillies/chiles (deseeded, if desired)

2 large garlic cloves, sliced

1 lemongrass stalk, trimmed and chopped

1 tsp ground turmeric

2 tbsp peanut oil

1 tbsp tamarind paste

1 tbsp light soy sauce

1 tbsp caster/superfine sugar

salt, to taste (optional)

MAKES 125 ML/ ½ CUP

Put the shallots, chillies, garlic, lemongrass and turmeric in a food processor and blend until smooth, adding 2 teaspoons of the oil if necessary.

Heat the remaining oil in a wok or large frying pan/skillet set over a very low heat and gently fry the paste for 10 minutes, until really fragrant. Stir in the tamarind paste, soy sauce and sugar and cook, stirring continuously, for 5 minutes until the oil comes to the top. Remove the pan from the heat and leave to cool completely.

Use as required or store in a sterilized glass bottle or jar in the fridge for up to 1 month.

SWEET & SOUR CHILLI SAUCE

This Burmese dressing is a simpler affair, but delicious nonetheless. It is delicious drizzled into soups but be sure to make plenty if you enjoy the taste – you'll soon be adding it to every meal.

15 g/3 tbsp chopped dried red chillies/chiles

4 garlic cloves, roughly chopped

2 tbsp fish sauce

2 tbsp soft brown sugar

50 ml/scant ¼ cup rice vinegar

MAKES 250 ML/ 1 CUP

Roughly crush the chillies in a pestle and mortar and transfer to a small saucepan with 75 ml/scant ⅓ cup cold water. Bring the mixture to the boil and simmer very gently over a low heat for 2 minutes, add the garlic and cook for a further 3 minutes.

Transfer the mixture to a food processor with the fish sauce and sugar, and blend until smooth. Add the vinegar and blend once more.

Pour the sauce into a sterilized glass bottle and seal. Store in the fridge for 2–3 days before using and then up to 1 month.

TIRK SALOUK SWAI

Much like the salsas of Mexico, the Caribbean and South America, this Cambodian mango salsa (opposite, front) makes use of the seasonal glut of fresh mangoes. It is at once sweet, salty and sour – quite delicious and lovely served alongside a seafood or chicken noodle salad.

1 large mango, peeled and chopped

juice of ½ lime

1 spring onion/ scallion, trimmed and finely chopped

2 tbsp chopped fresh coriander/ cilantro

1–2 large green chillies/chiles, deseeded and finely chopped

1–2 tsp fish sauce, to taste

SERVES 4

Put the mango flesh, lime juice, spring onion, coriander and chillies into a small mixing bowl. Stir well and season with fish sauce to taste. Serve at once.

JEOW MARG LENG

A Laotian cooked tomato salsa (opposite, back) that is wonderfully spicy and smoky. It works well alongside noodle salads.

6 large cherry tomatoes

6 garlic cloves, unpeeled

1 large shallot, unpeeled

1–2 small red bird's eye chillies/chiles

½ tsp caster/superfine sugar

1 spring onion/scallion, trimmed and finely chopped

1 tbsp chopped fresh coriander/cilantro

2 tsp lime juice

1 tsp fish sauce

SERVES 4

Heat a stovetop ridged grill pan over a medium heat until smoking and then grill the tomatoes for 15–20 minutes until completely charred and softened. Set aside to cool, then peel and discard the blackened skin. Repeat with the garlic cloves, whole shallot and chillies, cooking them until the skins are charred and the flesh softened. Allow them to cool, then peel and discard the skin.

Chop the vegetables and put them in a pestle and mortar. Pound to a rough paste. Transfer the paste to a mixing bowl and stir in the sugar, spring onion, coriander, lime juice and fish sauce and mix well.

Store in a sterilized glass jar in the fridge for up to 3 weeks and use as required.

BALACHUNG

A must-have condiment in Burmese cooking, this salty, spicy, crispy dish is served with almost every meal. It is delicious strewn over any noodle dish.

50 g/¼ cup dried shrimp

6 tbsp peanut (or vegetable) oil

2 Asian shallots, thinly sliced

2 garlic cloves, sliced

5 cm/2 inch piece of fresh ginger, peeled and thinly sliced

2–3 tsp dried red chilli/hot red pepper flakes

1 tbsp shrimp paste

MAKES ABOUT 55 G/¼ CUP

Grind the dried shrimp to a paste using a spice grinder or pestle and mortar and set aside.

Heat the oil in a wok set over a medium–high heat and fry the shallots for 4–5 minutes, until crisp and golden. Remove the shallots from the oil using a slotted spoon and drain on paper towels, leaving the pan over the heat.

Add the garlic, ginger and chilli flakes to the hot oil and cook for 2–3 minutes, until crisp and golden. Remove with a slotted spoon and drain on paper towels, again leaving the pan over the heat.

Stir in the ground dried shrimp and the shrimp paste and stir-fry for 2–3 minutes, until fragrant. Return the shallots and garlic mixture to the pan and stir gently until you a have a slightly sticky mixture. Cool completely before scattering over your favourite noodle dish.

The balachung can be stored in an airtight container for up to 2 weeks.

DEEP-FRIED SHALLOTS

Like balachung, deep-fried shallots are an integral part of Thai, as well as Vietnamese, Cambodian and Laotian cuisine, where they are sprinkled over numerous salads, soups, rice and noodle dishes. You can buy these from Asian stores for a quick alternative.

12 Asian shallots, thinly sliced

vegetable oil, for deep frying

MAKES ABOUT 50 G/ ⅓ CUP

Pour the oil into a wok or (old) saucepan about 5 cm/2 inches up the side of the pan and set over a medium heat. Test the temperature of the pan by dropping a cube of bread into the hot oil – it should crisp within 30 seconds.

Deep-fry the shallots, in batches, for 2–3 minutes, until crisp and golden, but do not allow the shallots to burn or they will become bitter. Remove with a slotted spoon and drain on paper towels.

Serve immediately or store in an airtight container for up to 2 weeks. If they become a little soggy, crisp them up in a dry frying pan/skillet as necessary.

Tip: Strain the leftover shallot oil through a fine mesh sieve/ strainer and use in salads and stir-fries.

ASIAN PICKLES

A mainstay of Asian cooking, in Japan pickles (opposite, left) are eaten as a snack, while in China pickled vegetables (opposite, right) are commonly served with noodle soups and salads. Kimchi (opposite, middle), a spiced pickled cabbage, is the national dish of Korea and is served with every meal.

JAPANESE PICKLED CUCUMBER

2 tsp salt

3 tbsp caster/superfine sugar

3 small cucumbers

2 x 500 ml/1 pint sterilized glass jars with airtight lids

MAKES 2 JARS

Combine the salt and sugar in a plastic container. Cut the cucumbers into 3-mm/⅛-inch thick slices on the diagonal and add to the salt mixture, stirring to coat evenly. Seal the container and store in the fridge for 3 days.

Remove from the fridge and taste a piece of cucumber to see if you like the pickle flavour. You can use immediately or continue to pickle them for a further day or two.

CHINESE PICKLED VEGETABLES

300 ml/1¼ cups white vinegar

200 g/1 cup caster/superfine sugar

1½ tsp salt

1 large carrot, cut into batons

1 celery stick/rib, cut into batons

½ cucumber, deseeded and cut into batons

a 500 ml/1 pint sterilized glass jar with airtight lid

MAKES 1 JAR

Put the vinegar, sugar and salt in a saucepan set over a low heat and warm through until the sugar is dissolved. Increase the heat, bring the mixture to the boil, simmer for 1 minute then remove from the heat.

Put the prepared vegetables in a large mixing bowl and pour over the syrup. Set aside until completely cool. Store in the fridge until ready to serve. These pickles can be made up to 3 days ahead.

QUICK KIMCHI

350 g/6 cups Chinese cabbage, thinly sliced

4 tsp sea salt

2 tbsp caster/superfine sugar

1 tbsp gochugaru (dried Korean chilli/chile flakes)

2 tsp freshly grated ginger

2 garlic cloves, crushed

2 tbsp fish sauce

2 tsp sesame seeds, toasted

2 spring onions/ scallions, trimmed and thinly sliced

a 500 ml/1 pint sterilized glass jar with airtight lid

MAKES 1 JAR

Put the cabbage in a bowl and stir in the salt. Add enough water to cover and leave to soak for 30 minutes. Drain and squeeze out excess water using a clean cloth.

Mix together the sugar, gochugaru, ginger, garlic, fish sauce and sesame seeds in a small bowl to make a thin paste.

Stir the paste into the cabbage with the spring onions, cover and leave to marinate for 1 hour. Serve, or store for up to 2 days in the fridge.

INDEX

RECIPE CREDITS

Dunja Gulin
Vegan Temaki Rolls with Seed Pate

Carol Hilker
Chinese Egg Rolls

Jenny Linford
Crispy Chicken Wontons
Garlic Pork Bao Buns

Loretta Liu
Barbecue Pork Puffs
Barbecue Pork Steamed Buns
Beef Bulgogi Puffs
Bok Choy Rolls with Spicy Chicken
Char Sui Steamed Buns
Chicken & Potato Cream Stew Dumplings
Chinese Vegetable Clamshell Buns
Clamshell Bao with Chicken Teriyaki
Clamshell Bao with Miso Salmon
Crab Dumplings
Duck Confit Puffs
Dumplings with Makrut Lime & Lemongrass
Fried Shrimp & Scallop Bao
Little Szechuan Chicken Steamed Buns
Lotus Leaf Rice Dumplings
Mixed Mushroom Puffs
Pea Shoot & Shrimp Dumplings
Peking-style Duck Pancake Wraps
Pork & Cabbage Shumai
Pork & Leek Jiaoizi
Pulled Pork & Olive Dumplings
Pumpkin & Leek Dumplings
Red Curry Chicken & Lentil Bao
Salmon & Asian Pesto Parcels
Salmon & Mushroom Dumplings
Scallop & Crab Dumplings
Shrimp & Mango Wontons
Spicy Chicken & Shrimp Dumplings
Steamed Buns Filled with Spicy Mala Lamb & Mint
Steamed Cabbage Leaf Spring Rolls
Steamed Flat Rice Noodle & Asparagus Rolls
Steamed Tofu Skin with Wild Mushroom Filling
Tofu, Sundried Tomato & Olive Dumplings
Vietnamese Vegetable Summer Rolls
Wonton Pork Moneybags

Elsa Petersen-Schepelern
Dumplings with Pepper Soy
Malaysian Fish Parcels
Rice Parcels

Louise Pickford
Asian Pickles
Balachung
Beef Bulgogi & Rice Noodle Wraps
Chinese & Japanese Dipping Sauces
Chinese Potstickers
Deep-fried Shallots
Green Nam Jim
Jeow Marg Leng
Kimchi Noodle Dumplings
Korean Dipping Sauces
Noodle-wrapped Prawns with Sweet Chilli Sauce
Nuoc Cham
Salmon & Spring Onion Gyoza
Sambal Olek
Smoked Duck Summer Rolls
Sweet & Sour Chilli Sauce
Szechuan Chilli Dressing
Tirk Salouk Swai
Vegetarian Spring Rolls
Wafu Dressing

PHOTOGRAPHY CREDITS

Peter Cassidy
Page 75

Louise Hagger
Pages 2, 5, 6, 12, 20, 28, 31, 33, 34, 37, 40, 51, 56, 64, 69, 79, 82, 86, 107,

Toby Scott
Page 93,

Ian Wallace
Pages 14, 23, 66, 73, 76, 89, 94, 112, 115, 116, 121, 125.

Clare Winfield
Pages 1, 3, 8, 17, 19, 24, 27, 43, 44, 47, 48, 53, 55, 59, 60, 70, 84, 90, 97, 99, 100, 103, 104.